Name:

Essential Exam Practice

Key Stage 4 Mathematics Higher Level

Ruso Bradley and June Hall

Introduction

We believe mathematics is a subject where practice is the key to exam success. There can be no better way of boosting your grade than practising the type of questions that will come up in your exams. It is no secret that many questions come up year after year, which is why the Essential Exam Practice range concentrates on these extremely important questions. It is also true that you can't predict exactly what will be in your exams, but we think that we have pretty much covered all the options!

About this book

This book is aimed at candidates taking the Higher tier in GCSE Mathematics, and is suitable for all examination boards.

The questions are split into four main sections:

- Number (N)
- Algebra (A)
- Shape, Space & Measures (S)
- Handling Data (H)

Within these sections, the questions are grouped by topic, so you can quickly find what you're looking for. Answers to all questions can be found at the back of the book, so you can check that you're on the right track.

Good luck in your exams!

Contents

Non-Calculator Questions

N1 A landscape gardener bought 486 garden shrubs, at 62p each, from a local garden centre.

(a) Without using a calculator and showing all your working, work out how much the landscape gardener spent on the shrubs.

Answer £ .... *(2 marks)*

The garden centre gives its customers an extra shrub free for every 18 bought.

(b) How many extra shrubs did the landscape gardener get?
Show all your working.

Answer .... *(2 marks)*

N2 DO NOT use a calculator for this question. Show all your working.

There were 713 runners in a half-marathon race. Each competitor had to pay 74p towards the cost of the first aid tent.

(a) How much, in total, did the runners contribute towards the first aid tent?

Answer £ .... *(2 marks)*

The organisers of the race were obliged to hire 1 safety marshal for every 23 competitors.

(b) How many safety marshals did they have to hire?

Answer .... *(2 marks)*

N3 The diagram shows an aeroplane 126 m above the sea and a submarine below the surface.

(a) How far is the sea bed below the aeroplane?

....

Answer ....m *(1 mark)*

The base of the submarine is 46 m above the sea bed.

(b) How far below sea level is the base of the submarine?

....

Answer ....m *(1 mark)*

N4

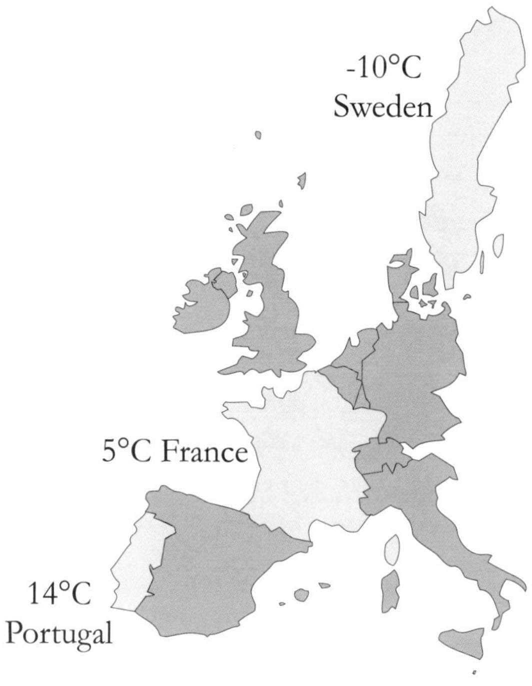

(a) According to the map, how much warmer is Portugal than Sweden?

....

Answer .... °C *(1 mark)*

(b) The temperatures drop to 10°C below those shown on the map.
What is the new temperature in:

Sweden ....°C

France .... °C *(2 marks)*

N5 A golf club has 360 members, 24 of which are junior members. What fraction of members are juniors? Reduce your answer to its lowest terms.

....

Answer .... *(2 marks)*

N6 During November it snowed on 5 days. On what fraction of days in November did snow fall? Reduce your answer to its lowest terms.

....

Answer .... *(2 marks)*

Non-Calculator Questions

N7 **(a)** Convert 0.15 into a fraction in its lowest terms.

....

Answer .... *(2 marks)*

(b) Write down the value of 0.15×100.

Answer .... *(1 mark)*

(c) Write down the value of $0.15 \div 100$.

Answer .... *(1 mark)*

(d) What is $(2 - 10) \div (-1 + \frac{3}{4})$?

....

Answer .... *(2 marks)*

Multiples & Factors

N8 From the list of numbers 2, 4, 6, 9, 10, 11, write down

(a) all the multiples of 2

Answer .... *(1 mark)*

(b) all the factors of 10

Answer .... *(1 mark)*

x and y are two different numbers from the list.
x is a factor of 10 and y is a multiple of 3.

$x = \frac{5}{3}y$

(c) Find x and y.

....

Answer $x =$ ...., $y =$ .... *(2 marks)*

Multiples & Factors

N9 **(a)** Find the lowest common multiple of 12, 21 and 42.

....

Answer ....*(1 mark)*

(b) Find the highest common factor of 12, 16 and 24.

....

....

Answer ....*(1 mark)*

N10 **(a)** Find the lowest common multiple of 50 and 85.

....

....

Answer ....*(1 mark)*

(b) Find the highest common factor of 720 and 84.

....

....

Answer ....*(1 mark)*

N11 Calculate the smallest length of rope that can be cut into an exact number of 4 m lengths, 7 m lengths or 14 m lengths.

....

....

Answer .... m *(2 marks)*

N12 Calculate the smallest length of string that can be cut into an exact number of 3 cm lengths, 6 cm lengths or 8 cm lengths.

....

....

Answer .... cm *(2 marks)*

N13 A wooden box full of coffee beans weighs 40 kg. The coffee beans themselves weigh 35 kg.

(a) What percentage of the total weight is the weight of the coffee beans?

....

Answer .... % *(2 marks)*

(b) What percentage of the total weight is the weight of the wooden box?

....

Answer .... % *(1 mark)*

N14 Out of 32 teams in a basketball tournament, 20 of them play in red shorts.

(a) What percentage of teams play in red shorts?

....

Answer .... % *(2 marks)*

(b) What percentage of teams do not play in red shorts?

....

Answer .... % *(1 mark)*

N15 John and Raana share £39 in the ratio 5:8. What is John's share?

....

....

Answer £ .... *(2 marks)*

N16 **(a)** Anthony and Sarah share £55 in the ratio 4:7. What is Sarah's share?

....

....

Answer £ .... *(2 marks)*

(b) What percentage of the money belongs to Anthony?

....

....

Answer .... % *(2 marks)*

N17 At a timber merchants, pine costs £20 per cubic foot.

(a) Oak costs 15% more per cubic foot than pine.
How much, per cubic foot, does oak cost?

....

Answer £ .... *(2 marks)*

(b) Mahogany costs 25% more than oak.
How much, per cubic foot, is mahogany?

....

Answer £ .... *(2 marks)*

N18 Red grapes cost £1.90 per kg. White grapes cost 20% more.
How much do white grapes cost?

....

Answer £ .... per kg *(2 marks)*

N19 A chocolate cake for 5 people requires 75 g of sugar.
Daphne makes a chocolate cake for 8 people.

(a) Calculate the weight of sugar that Daphne needs.

....

Answer .... g *(2 marks)*

(b) Daphne cuts the cake into 8 equal slices. Her friends eat 5 slices of the cake.
What percentage of the cake is left?

....

Answer .... % *(2 marks)*

N20 A pizza for 7 people requires 840 g of flour. Dennis makes a pizza for 4 people.

(a) Calculate the weight of flour that Dennis needs for his pizza.

....

Answer .... g *(2 marks)*

(b) Dennis eats 1 person's share of the pizza.
What percentage of the pizza is left?

....

Answer .... % *(2 marks)*

N21 A new car is on sale for £12 000. Given that the car's value will decrease by 15% each year,

(a) how much will the car be worth after 1 year?

....

Answer £... *(2 marks)*

(b) how much will the car be worth after 2 years?

....

Answer £... *(2 marks)*

N22 David deposits £40 in a savings account that offers a return of 6% per annum.
If David doesn't make any further deposits or withdrawals,

(a) how much money will be in the account after 1 year?

....

Answer £... *(2 marks)*

(b) how much money will be in the account after 2 years?

....

Answer £... *(2 marks)*

Number

Percentages & Ratios

N23 A double glazing manufacturer reduced the price of their most expensive front door from £620 to £540. What was the percentage reduction in price?

....

Answer .... % *(2 marks)*

N24 Shortly after 25 December, the price of tinsel dropped from £2.10 to £1.60. What was the percentage reduction in price?

....

Answer .... % *(2 marks)*

N25 A house rose in value by 15% to £72 000 over the last year.

(a) What was the value of the house a year ago?

....

Answer £ .... *(3 marks)*

The value of a similar house dropped by 5% to £68 000 over the same period.

(b) What was the value of this house a year ago?

....

Answer £ .... *(3 marks)*

N26 A bottle of vintage wine has risen in value by 10% to £1200 over the last five years.

(a) How much was the bottle of wine worth five years ago?

....

Answer £ .... *(3 marks)*

In fact, at £1200 the wine is now worth 5% more than it was a year ago.

(b) How much was the wine worth a year ago?

....

Answer £ .... *(3 marks)*

Percentages & Ratios

N27 The width of a square is increased by 15%. Calculate the percentage change in the area of the square.

....

....

....

Answer ....% *(3 marks)*

N28 The base of a triangle is increased in size by 10% and the height by 20%. Calculate the percentage increase in the area of the triangle.

....

....

....

....

Answer ....% *(4 marks)*

Powers & Roots

N29 Find the values of the following numbers, correct to the accuracy given in brackets.

(a) 1.3^6 (3 significant figures)

Answer ....*(1 mark)*

(b) $10^{1/5}$ (2 decimal places)

Answer ....*(1 mark)*

(c) $\left(\frac{4}{3}\right)^{-3}$ (3 significant figures)

Answer ....*(1 mark)*

Powers & Roots

N30 Work out the following. Show your working and give your answers without indices.

(a) $8^{-\frac{1}{3}}$

....

Answer .... *(1 mark)*

(b) $16^{\frac{1}{4}} \times 32^{\frac{2}{5}}$

....

Answer .... *(1 mark)*

(c) $\dfrac{(5^2)^4}{25^3}$

....

Answer .... *(1 mark)*

N31 Given that $a^{5/2} \times a^{-3} \times \sqrt{a} = a^y$, find the value of y. Show all your working.

....

....

....

Answer y = ... *(2 marks)*

N32 DO NOT use a calculator for this question.
Find the value of x that satisfies $4^{-2} \times 2^{-x} = \dfrac{1}{2^6}$.

....

....

....

Answer x = ... *(3 marks)*

N33 Below is a list of numbers.

7, 9, 10, 12, 16, 27

(a) Which number is a cube number?

Answer .... *(1 mark)*

(b) Which two numbers are square numbers?

Answer .... *(2 marks)*

(c) Which number is a triangular number?

Answer .... *(2 marks)*

(d) From the list, find two numbers x and y such that $\frac{x^2}{3} = y$.

....

....

Answer x = ..., y = ... *(2 marks)*

N34 x, y and z are different numbers in this list:

3, 7, 9, 12, 13, 15, 16

x is a triangular number.
y is a prime number.
z is a square number.
$x + y = z$

Work out the values of x, y and z.

....

....

Answer x = ...

y = ...

z = ... *(2 marks)*

Primes & Prime Factorisation

N35 The prime factorisation of a certain number is

$$2^2 \times 3^2 \times 7$$

(a) Write down the number.

Answer ....*(1 mark)*

(b) What is the prime factorisation of 90?

....

Answer .... *(2 marks)*

N36 **(a)** Write 275 as a product of its prime factors.

....

....

Answer .... *(2 marks)*

(b) The prime factorisation of 180 can be written in the form

$$2^x \times 3^y \times 5^z$$

Find x, y and z.

....

....

....

Answer x = ...

y = ...

z = ... *(2 marks)*

N37 **(a)** The list below contains rational and irrational numbers.
Pick out all the irrational numbers.

$2\pi,\ 1.\dot{2}\dot{3},\ \frac{5}{7},\ \sqrt{12},\ \sqrt{9},\ \frac{\sqrt{12}}{\sqrt{3}}$

Answer .... *(2 marks)*

(b) Find a number that lies between 14 and 15 and has a rational square root.

....

Answer .... *(2 marks)*

(c) Give two different irrational numbers that have a rational product.

....

Answer .... *(2 marks)*

N38 **(a)** From the list below, write down all the rational numbers.

$\frac{4\pi}{3},\ \frac{3}{5},\ 11.2,\ \sqrt{6},\ \frac{\sqrt{15}}{\sqrt{3}},\ \pi^2$

Answer .... *(2 marks)*

(b) Write down a number that lies between 10 and 15 and has a rational cube root.

....

Answer .... *(2 marks)*

(c) x and y are two irrational numbers, such that $xy = 12$. Write down a value for x and a corresponding value for y.

....

Answer $x =$ ...., $y =$ .... *(2 marks)*

RATIONAL, IRRATIONAL & SURDS

N39 Write $0.\dot{3}\dot{1}$ in the form $\frac{a}{b}$, where a and b are positive integers.

Answer .... *(3 marks)*

N40 Write $0.\dot{4}2\dot{6}$ in the form $\frac{a}{b}$, where a and b are positive integers.

Answer .... *(3 marks)*

N41 **(a)** Express $\frac{6}{\sqrt{2}}$ in the form $a\sqrt{b}$, where a and b are integers.

Answer .... *(2 marks)*

(b) Simplify the following. Give your answer in the form $p + q\sqrt{3}$, where p and q are integers.

$(2 + \sqrt{3})(4 - \sqrt{3})$

Answer .... *(3 marks)*

N42 Convert the improper fraction $\frac{8}{7}$ to a decimal correct to:

(a) 2 decimal places

Answer ....(*1 mark*)

(b) 2 significant figures

Answer ....(*1 mark*)

N43 Convert the improper fraction $\frac{11}{9}$ to a decimal correct to:

(a) 3 decimal places

Answer ....(*1 mark*)

(b) 3 significant figures

Answer ....(*1 mark*)

N44 **(a)** Find an approximate value for the expression: $\frac{20.3 \times 51.2}{498.6}$

....

Answer .... (*2 marks*)

(b) The entire surface of a sphere of radius 5.2 m is to be painted.
There is enough paint to cover 280 m^2.

Use approximations to estimate whether there is enough paint to cover the sphere.
(Surface area of a sphere = $4\pi r^2$)

....

.... (*3 marks*)

N45 **(a)** Find an approximate value for the expression: $\frac{409.2 \times 0.523}{41.6}$

....

Answer .... (*2 marks*)

Rounding & Estimating

(b) The entire surface of the cube shown is to be painted.
There is enough paint to cover 5000 cm^2.

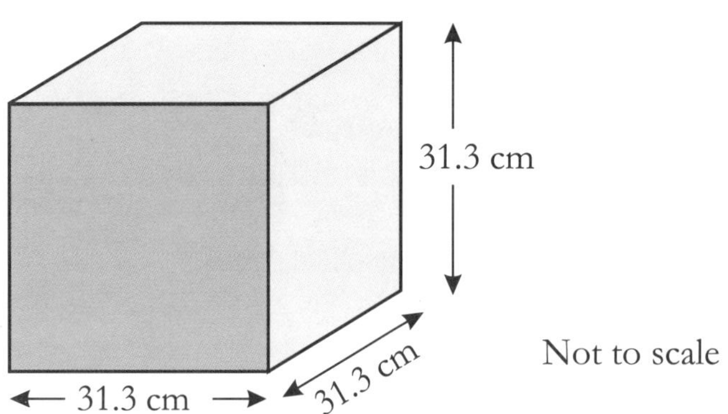

Use approximations to estimate whether there is enough paint.

....

.... *(3 marks)*

N46 Calculate, giving your answer to an appropriate degree of accuracy:

$$\frac{29.42 \times 0.0941}{15.2 \times 8.42}$$

....

Answer .... *(2 marks)*

N47 Calculate, giving your answer to an appropriate degree of accuracy:

$$\frac{9.59 \times 0.024}{7.2 \times 1.4}$$

....

Answer .... *(2 marks)*

Conversions

N48 Given that 1 mile is approximately 1.6 km, which distance is the greatest: 15 miles or 25 000 metres?

....

Answer .... *(2 marks)*

N49 Which is the heaviest, 110 pounds or 47 000 g?
(1 kilogram is approximately equal to 2.2 lbs)

....

Answer .... *(2 marks)*

N50 Before his holiday, Ivan exchanged £400 for $560.

(a) Anne changed £300 into dollars at the same exchange rate.
How many dollars did Anne get in return?

....

....

Answer $ .... *(3 marks)*

(b) Ivan bought a pair of sunglasses for $40.
What was the cost of the sunglasses in pounds?

....

Answer £ .... *(2 marks)*

N51 Ali exchanged £750 for Drc304 500 before travelling to Greece.

(a) Harvey changed £600 into drachmas at the same exchange rate.
How many drachmas did Harvey get in return?

....

....

Answer Drc .... *(3 marks)*

(b) Ali bought a swimming costume for Drc1800.
What was the price of the swimming costume in pounds?

....

Answer £ .... *(2 marks)*

Algebra

Standard Index Form

A1 **(a)** Write 920 000 in standard form.

Answer ....*(1 mark)*

(b) Write 4.3×10^6 as an ordinary number.

Answer ....*(1 mark)*

A2 Work out the following, leaving your answer in standard form.

(a) $(4.1 \times 10^5) + (3.2 \times 10^4)$

....

Answer .... *(2 marks)*

(b) $(6.4 \times 10^6) - (3 \times 10^4)$

....

Answer .... *(2 marks)*

A3 The population of India is roughly 850 million. India's surface area is approximately 3×10^6 km^2.

(a) Write the population of India in standard form.

Answer ....*(1 mark)*

(b) Calculate the approximate average area, in km^2, per head of population. Give your answer in standard form.

....

Answer .... km^2 *(2 marks)*

A4 The Moon is 384 000 km from the Earth's surface.
The diameter of the Moon is 3.5×10^3 km.

(a) Write the distance between the Moon and the Earth in standard form.

Answer ....km *(1 mark)*

(b) In terms of the diameter of the Moon, how far is the Moon from the Earth?

....

Answer .... Moon diameters *(2 marks)*

A5 One volume of an encyclopedia contains 6.2×10^2 pages, printed on both sides.

(a) The thickness of a page is 7.4×10^{-3} cm.
Disregarding the cover, what is the thickness of the encyclopedia?

....

....

Answer .... cm *(2 marks)*

(b) Without the cover, the encyclopedia weighs 4.2×10^2 g.
What is the weight of a single page?

....

....

Answer .... g *(2 marks)*

A6 The Arctic Ocean has a surface area of 1.4×10^7 km^2 and an average depth of 1.3×10^3 m.
The Pacific Ocean has a surface area of 1.8×10^8 km^2 and an average depth of 4.3×10^3 m.

(a) In terms of surface area, how many times bigger is the Pacific Ocean than the Arctic Ocean?

....

....

Answer .... *(2 marks)*

(b) On average, how many times deeper is the Pacific Ocean than the Arctic Ocean?

....

....

Answer .... *(2 marks)*

Forming & Solving Equations

A7 Solve the equations:

(a) $\frac{5}{3}x = 2$

....

Answer $x =$ ....*(1 mark)*

(b) $15 - 3x = 3$

....

....

Answer $x =$ .... *(2 marks)*

(c) $16 - 2x = 4x + 10$

....

....

Answer $x =$ .... *(2 marks)*

(d) $4(2x - 1) = 7x + 11$

....

....

....

Answer $x =$ .... *(3 marks)*

(e) $\frac{180}{x + 3} = 12$

....

....

....

Answer $x =$ .... *(3 marks)*

A8 Solve the following equations:

(a) $\frac{11}{9}y = 5$

....

Answer $y =$ ....(*1 mark*)

(b) $11 - 6y = -1$

....

....

Answer $y =$ .... (*2 marks*)

(c) $14 + 9y = 5y + 26$

....

....

Answer $y =$ .... (*2 marks*)

(d) $3(5y + 6) = 20y + 8$

....

....

....

Answer $y =$ .... (*3 marks*)

(e) $\frac{150}{y + 3} = 10$

....

....

....

Answer $y =$ .... (*3 marks*)

Forming & Solving Equations

A9 Peri bought 4 books and a bedside lamp from a jumble sale. The lamp cost £8 and he spent £32 in total.

(a) If each book cost £x, write down an equation in x.

Answer .... *(2 marks)*

(b) Solve your equation to find the cost of one book.

....

....

Answer £ .... *(2 marks)*

A10 Dan buys 4 jars of garlic and a pot of ground coriander from the supermarket. The pot of coriander weighs 12 g. The whole bag of shopping weighs 852 g.

(a) Write down an equation in y, where y represents the weight of one jar of garlic.

Answer .... *(2 marks)*

(b) Solve the equation for y and hence write down the weight of 1 jar of garlic.

....

....

Answer .... g *(2 marks)*

Substituting Values

A11 If $x = 3$ and $y = 2\frac{1}{2}$, what is the value of:

(a) $2xy$

....

Answer .... *(2 marks)*

(b) $3x^2 + 2y$

....

Answer .... *(2 marks)*

A12 Given that $A = 3$ and $B = \frac{2}{3}$, work out the value of:

(a) $\frac{AB}{A^2}$

....

....

Answer .... *(2 marks)*

(b) $A(B + A)$

....

....

Answer .... *(2 marks)*

A13 The time needed to cook a turkey is given as 20 minutes per pound plus an extra 20 minutes.

(a) Write down a formula for the time taken, T, to cook a turkey of weight W lb.

Answer $T =$ .... *(2 marks)*

(b) How many hours will a turkey weighing 8 lb take to cook?

....

....

Answer .... hours *(2 marks)*

A14 A salesman is paid according to how many hours he works and the number of products he sells.

(a) If he receives £6 per hour plus £2 for every item sold, write down a formula for his pay, P, in terms of hours worked, H, and number of items sold, S.

Answer $P =$ £ .... *(2 marks)*

Substituting Values

(b) How much does the salesman get paid if he works 7 hours and sells 15 items?

....

Answer £ .... *(2 marks)*

Rearranging Formulae

A15 Make a the subject of the formula $b = a^2 + 2$.

....

Answer $a =$ .... *(2 marks)*

A16 Rearrange the formula $4 + 3x = y^{1/3}$, so that x is the subject.

....

Answer $x =$ .... *(2 marks)*

A17 You are given the formula $a = 2bc^2$.

(a) Rearrange the formula to give b in terms of a and c.

....

Answer $b =$ .... *(2 marks)*

(b) Rearrange the formula to give c in terms of a and b.

....

....

Answer $c =$ .... *(2 marks)*

A18 $v^2 = u^2 + 2as$ is a formula used in physics.

(a) Rearrange the formula to give a in terms of u, v and s.

....

....

Answer $a =$ .... *(2 marks)*

Rearranging Formulae

(b) Rearrange the formula to give u in terms of v, a and s.

....

....

Answer u = ... *(2 marks)*

Algebraic Fractions

A19 **(a)** Express $\dfrac{9x^3 \times 4x^3}{12x^2}$ as simply as possible.

....

Answer .... *(2 marks)*

(b) Combine as a single fraction $\dfrac{x}{3} + \dfrac{x^2}{6}$.

....

Answer .... *(2 marks)*

(c) Solve the equation $1 + \dfrac{2}{x} = 3$.

....

....

Answer x = ... *(3 marks)*

A20 Simplify:

(a) $\dfrac{x^3}{x} - \dfrac{x^2}{2}$

....

Answer .... *(2 marks)*

(b) $\dfrac{5x^4 \times 4x^3}{10x^5}$

....

Answer .... *(2 marks)*

(c) Solve the following equation: $\frac{3x}{2} - 6 = \frac{x}{2}$

....

....

Answer $x =$ .... *(3 marks)*

A21 **(a)** Make a the subject of the formula.

$$b = \frac{a + c}{ac}$$

....

....

....

Answer $a =$ .... *(3 marks)*

(b) Write the following as a single fraction:

$$\frac{4}{x + 2} + \frac{9}{x - 3}$$

....

....

....

....

Answer .... *(3 marks)*

A22 **(a)** Make x the subject of the equation.

$$\frac{1}{xy} + \frac{1}{x} = z$$

....

....

....

Answer $x =$ .... *(3 marks)*

(b) Write the following as a single fraction:

$$\frac{10}{x+1} - \frac{4}{2x+1}$$

....

....

....

....

Answer .... *(3 marks)*

A23 **(a)** At what value does the graph of $y = 2.5 - 0.5x$ cross the y-axis?

Answer $y =$ ....*(1 mark)*

(b) What is the gradient of the graph $y = 2.5 - 0.5x$?

Answer ....*(1 mark)*

(c) Draw the graph of $y = 2.5 - 0.5x$ for values of x between -3 and 3.

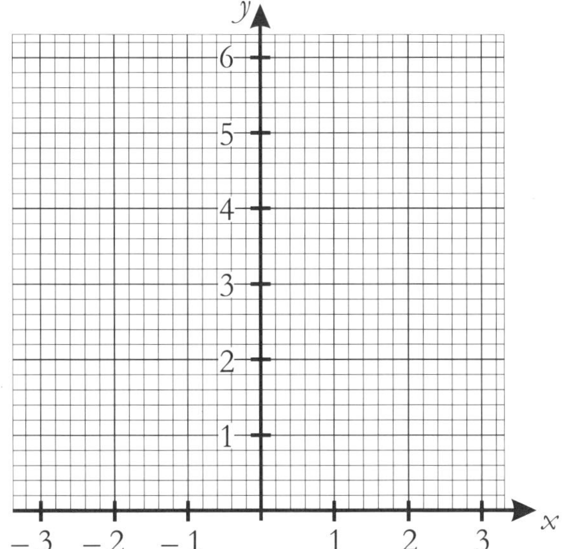

(2 marks)

Straight Lines

A24 **(a)** Draw the graph of $y = \frac{5}{2}x - 2$ for values of x from 0 to 6.

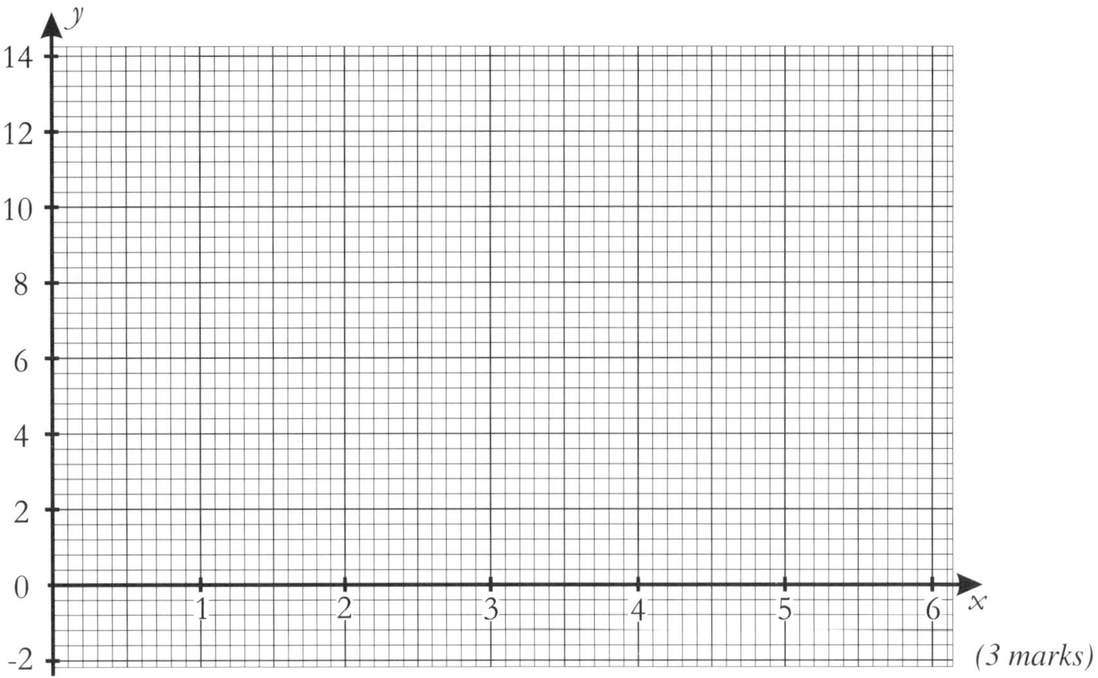

(3 marks)

(b) What is the value of y when $x = 4$?

Answer $y =$ ....*(1 mark)*

(c) What is the value of x when $y = 11$?

Answer $x =$ ....*(1 mark)*

A25 The cost of hiring a taxi includes a fixed amount and a charge per mile travelled, and is shown in the graph below.

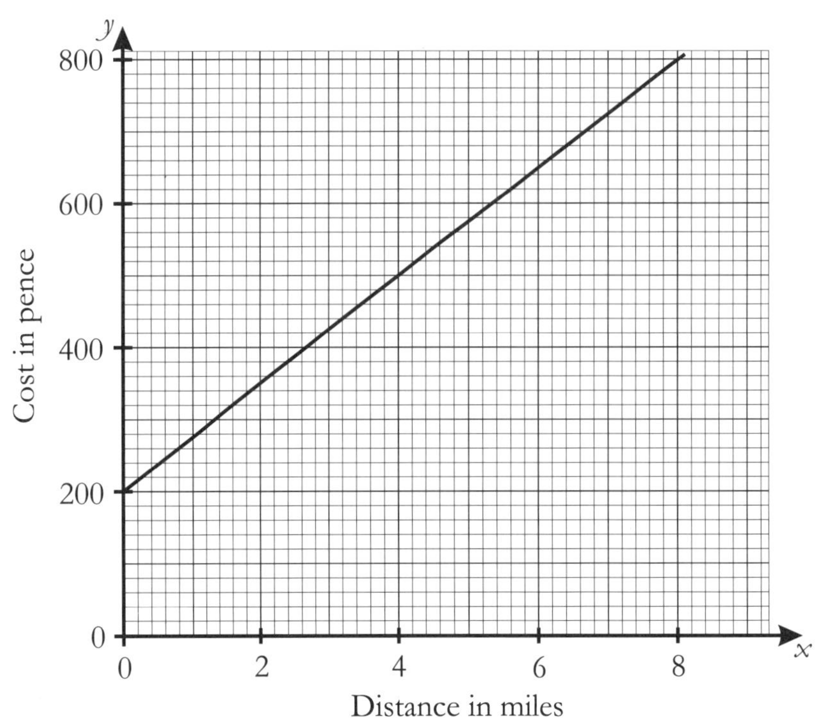

(a) Find the equation of the line in the form $y = ax + b$.

....

....

....

Answer $y =$ .... *(3 marks)*

(b) Calculate the cost of travelling 10 miles in the taxi.

....

....

Answer £ .... *(2 marks)*

A26 (a) Which of these lines is parallel to the the line with equation $2x - 4y = 4$?

$y = 4x - 3$	$3y = 6x - 4$	$y + 4x = 3$
$2y + 4x = 3$	$2 = 2x - y$	$6y = 3x + 8$

....

....

Answer .... *(2 marks)*

(b) Which of the lines is perpendicular to the the line with equation $x - 2y = 6$?

....

....

Answer .... *(2 marks)*

STRAIGHT LINES

A27 A line passes through the point (4, 9) and is parallel to the line with equation $y = 3x + 1$. Find the equation of the line.

....

....

....

Answer .... *(3 marks)*

A28 A line passes through the point (4, 1) and is perpendicular to the line with equation $y = \frac{1}{4}x - 12$. Find the equation of the line.

....

....

....

Answer .... *(3 marks)*

A29 The table below shows the mass (M, grams) of an ice cube at certain times (T, minutes).

Time (T, minutes)	1	2	3	4	5
Mass (M, grams)	9.2	7.8	6.6	5.7	4.9
0.8^T					

It is suggested that an equation for the relationship between M and T is

$$M = a(0.8)^T + b$$

(a) Complete the missing row in the table. *(1 mark)*

(b) On the graph paper below, plot a graph of M against 0.8^T.

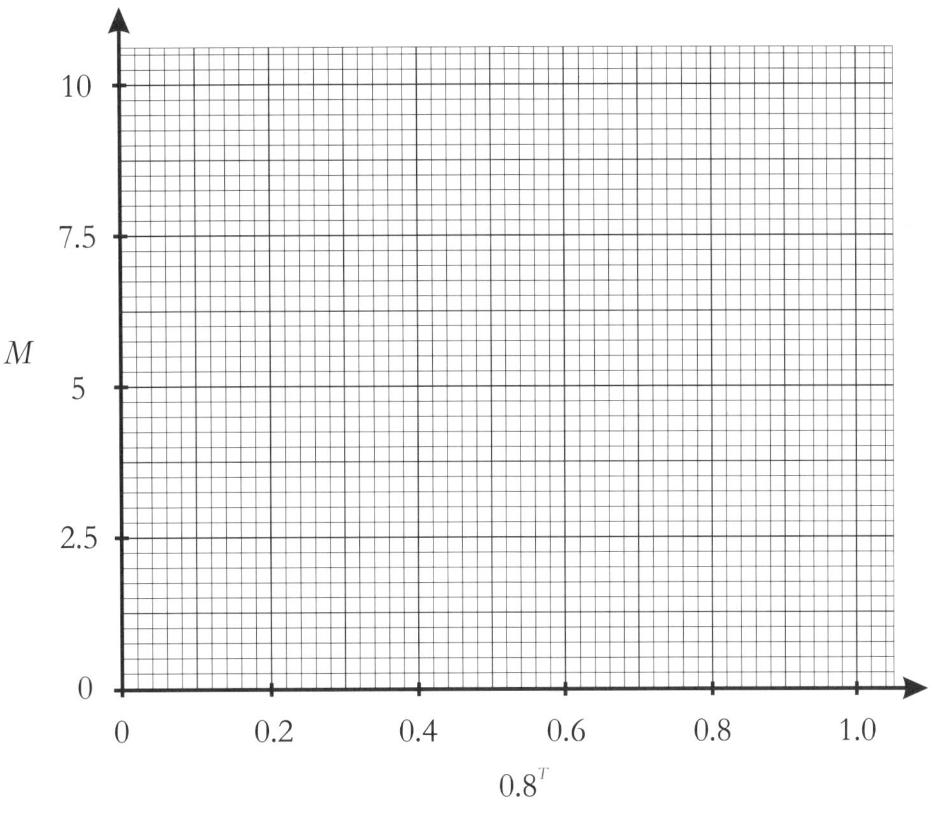

(2 marks)

(c) Use your graph to estimate the values of a and b.

....

....

Answer a = ... b = ... *(3 marks)*

(d) Using the fact that $0.8^0 = 1$, estimate the mass of the ice cube at the start.

....

....

Answer .... g *(2 marks)*

Algebra

Simultaneous Equations

A30 Solve algebraically the simultaneous equations below.

$$4x + 7y = 10$$
$$2x + 3y = 3$$

....

....

....

....

Answer $x =$ ...., $y =$ .... *(3 marks)*

A31 Solve algebraically:

$$9x + 11y = 15$$
$$4x + 4y = 4$$

....

....

....

....

Answer $x =$ ...., $y =$ .... *(3 marks)*

A32 **(a)** Solve the simultaneous equations: $3x - 5y = 1$
$2x + 3y = 7$

....

....

....

....

Answer $x =$ ...., $y =$ .... *(3 marks)*

(b) Draw the graphs of:

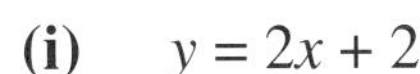

(i) $y = 2x + 2$

(ii) $y = 10 - 2x$

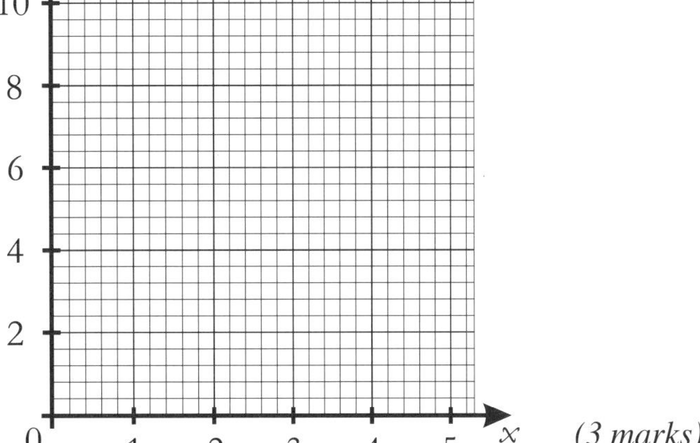

(3 marks)

(iii) Write down the value of x where the graphs meet.

Answer x = ... *(1 mark)*

A33 (a) Obtain a solution to the following simultaneous equations:

$$4x + 2y = 14$$
$$x + 3y = 6$$

....

....

....

....

Answer x = ..., y = ... *(3 marks)*

(b) Draw the graphs of:

(i) $y = 2x$

(ii) $y = 6 - x$

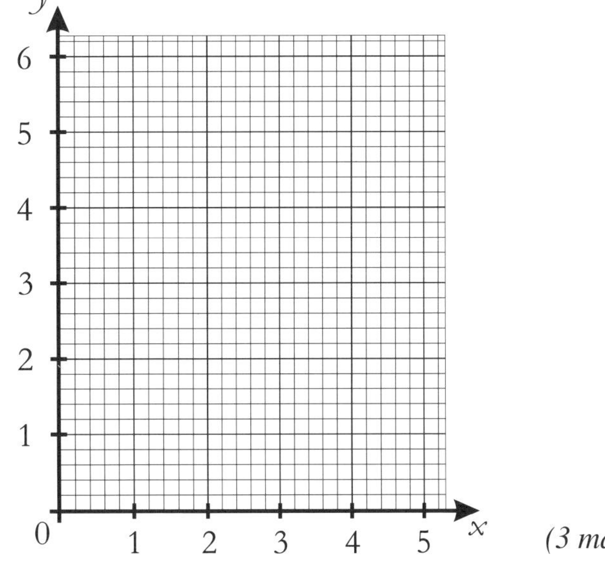

(3 marks)

(iii) Write down the value of y where the graphs meet.

Answer y = ... *(1 mark)*

A34 **(a)** Write down the equation of the circle.

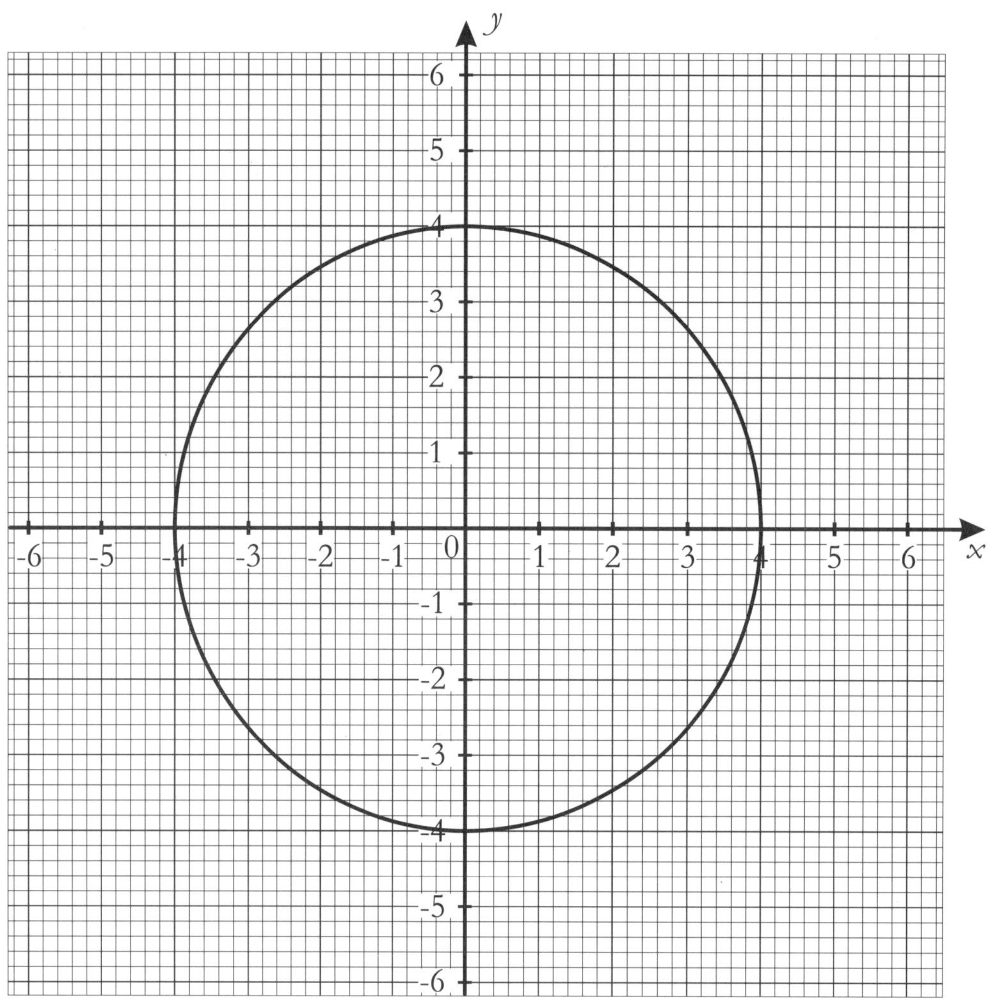

Answer .... *(2 marks)*

(b) By drawing a suitable line on the graph, find the coordinates of the points of intersection of the circle and the line $y = 4 - x$.

Answer (.........., ...), (..........., ...)*(2 marks)*

A35 Find the coordinates of the points of intersection of the line and circle.

$$y = 5 - \tfrac{1}{3}x$$

$$x^2 + y^2 = 25$$

....

....

....

....

....

....

....

....

Answer (.........., ...), (.........., ...) *(5 marks)*

A36 Find the coordinates of the points of intersection of the line and curve.

$$y = 2x - 9$$

$$y = x^2 - 3x - 3$$

....

....

....

....

....

....

....

....

Answer (.........., ...), (.........., ...) *(5 marks)*

INEQUALITIES

A37 List all the possible values of x such that $-5 \leqslant x < 4$, where x is an integer.

.... *(2 marks)*

A38 Write down all the values of x that satisfy $-2 < x \leqslant 6$, where x is an integer.

.... *(2 marks)*

A39 **(a)** Solve the inequality $3(4x + 3) < 15$.

....

....

....

Answer .... *(2 marks)*

(b) By first drawing three straight lines on the graph paper below, shade the region that satisfies

$$y > 1, \quad y \leqslant x \text{ and } x < 3.$$

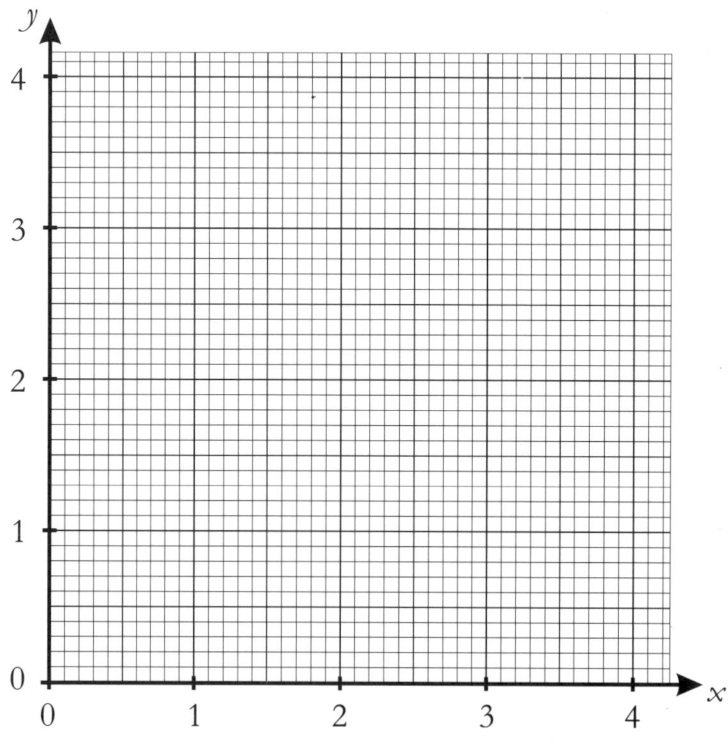

(3 marks)

A40 (a) Solve the inequality $5(3x - 7) < 5 + 2x$.

....

....

....

Answer .... *(2 marks)*

(b) On the graph paper provided, shade the region that satisfies

$$x < 6, \quad y < 5, \quad y + 2x > 6 \text{ and } y > x.$$

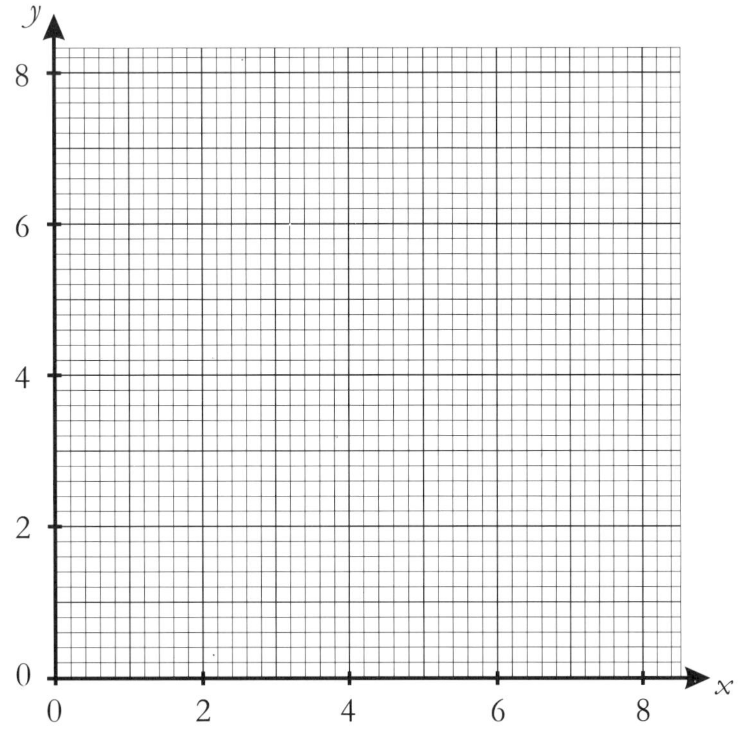

(4 marks)

(c) List the points with whole number coordinates that satisfy all four inequalities.

Answer ....*(1 mark)*

Trial & Improvement

A41 Showing all your trials, use trial and improvement to solve the following:

(a) $x^2 = 7$ (Give your answer correct to 1 decimal place.)

....

....

....

....

Answer $x =$ .... *(3 marks)*

(b) $x^3 + 2x = 5$ (Giving your answer correct to 1 decimal place.)

....

....

....

....

....

Answer $x =$ .... *(3 marks)*

A42 Using trial and improvement, solve the following equations:

(a) $x^2 = 19$ (to 1 d.p.)

....

....

....

....

Answer $x =$ .... *(3 marks)*

(b) $2x^3 - x = 11$ (to 1 d.p.)

....

....

....

....

....

Answer $x =$ .... *(3 marks)*

EXPANSION & FACTORISATION

A43 **(a)** Multiply out the brackets and simplify the expression $(2x + 9)(x - 7)$.

....

Answer .... *(2 marks)*

(b) Multiply out the brackets and collect together like terms.

$$x(2x^2 + 3) + x^2(x + 2) + x(x + 3)$$

....

....

Answer .... *(2 marks)*

(c) Factorise $x^2 + 5x + 6$.

....

....

Answer .... *(2 marks)*

Algebra

Expansion & Factorisation

A44 **(a)** Simplify, by first multiplying out the brackets: $(3x - 2)(5x + 4)$

....

Answer .... *(2 marks)*

(b) Simplify the following expression: $x(x + 2) + x^2(x + 2) + x(x^2 + 1)$

....

....

Answer .... *(2 marks)*

(c) Factorise $x^2 + 2x - 8$.

....

....

Answer .... *(2 marks)*

A45 Factorise $9x^2 - 16y^2$.

....

....

Answer .... *(2 marks)*

A46 Factorise $x^2 - 9y^2$.

....

....

Answer .... *(2 marks)*

A47 Complete the square on $x^2 + 6x + 12$.

....

....

Answer .... *(2 marks)*

Expansion & Factorisation

A48 $x^2 - 14x + 10$ can be written in the form $(x - a)^2 - b$. Find the values of a and b.

....

....

Answer a = ..., b = ... *(2 marks)*

Quadratics

A49 Solve $x^2 - 4x = 0$.

....

....

Answer x = ... *(2 marks)*

A50 Solve $x^2 + 3x = 0$.

....

....

Answer x = ... *(2 marks)*

A51 Solve $x^2 - x - 12 = 0$.

....

....

Answer x = ... *(3 marks)*

A52 Find both solutions to $x^2 - 3x - 10 = 0$.

....

....

Answer x = ... *(3 marks)*

Algebra

QUADRATICS

A53 These two rectangles have the same area:

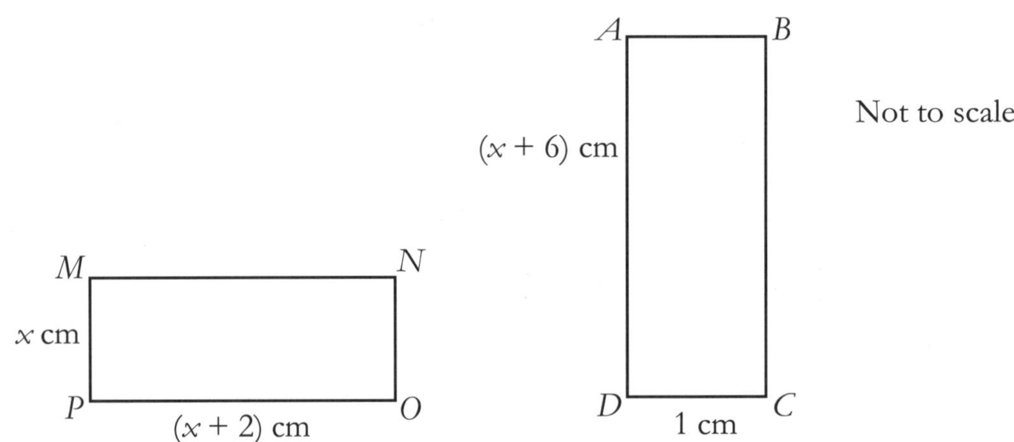

(a) Form an equation in x and show that it can be simplified to $x^2 + x - 6 = 0$.

....

....

.... *(2 marks)*

(b) Solve the equation $x^2 + x - 6 = 0$ to find the length of MP.

....

....

....

....

Answer MP = ... cm *(4 marks)*

A54 The perimeter of a rectangle is 32 cm and its length is x cm.

(a) Find an expression for the width of the rectangle in terms of x.

....

Answer .... cm *(2 marks)*

(b) Using the fact that the area of the rectangle is 48 cm², form an equation involving x and show that it can be simplified to $x^2 - 16x + 48 = 0$.

....

.... *(2 marks)*

(c) Solve the equation $x^2 - 16x + 48 = 0$ to find the 2 possible lengths of the rectangle.

....

....

....

Answer .... *(3 marks)*

A55 The lengths of the sides of a right-angled triangle are as shown:

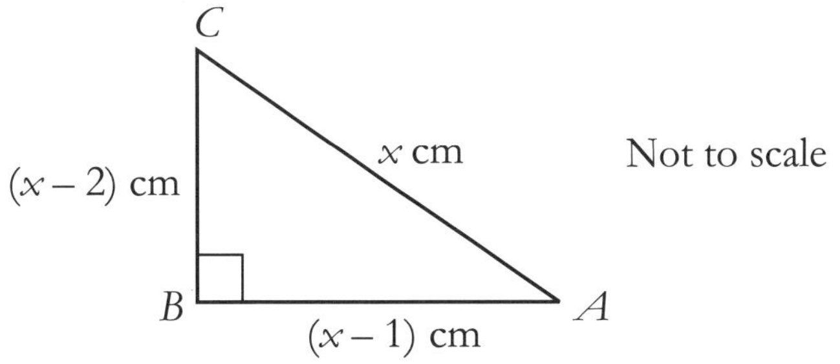

C

$(x - 2)$ cm

x cm

Not to scale

B

$(x - 1)$ cm

A

(a) Using Pythagoras' theorem, form and simplify a quadratic equation in x.

....

....

....

Answer .... *(3 marks)*

(b) Solve the equation to find an appropriate length for the hypotenuse.

....

....

....

....

Answer .... cm *(4 marks)*

A56 A right-angled triangle has sides of length x cm, $(x - 1)$ cm and $(x - 8)$ cm.

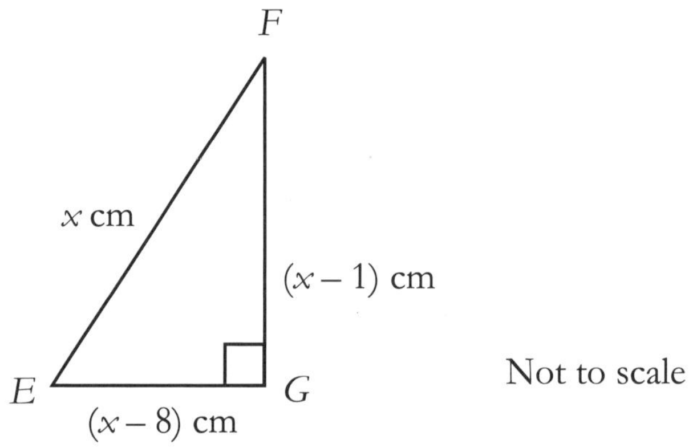

F

x cm

$(x - 1)$ cm

E G

$(x - 8)$ cm

Not to scale

(a) Form an equation in x and show that it simplifies to $x^2 - 18x + 65 = 0$.

....

....

.... *(3 marks)*

(b) Solve the equation and hence find the length of the hypotenuse.

....

....

....

....

Answer .... cm *(4 marks)*

A57 Find the solutions to $3x^2 - 5x + 1 = 0$. Give your answers correct to 2 d.p.

....

....

....

x = ... or x = ... *(3 marks)*

A58 Find both solutions of $4x^2 + 9x - 2 = 0$. Give your answers to 3 sig. figs.

....

....

....

x = ... or x = ... *(3 marks)*

A59 **(a)** Complete the table of values for $y = 4x^2 - 4x - 3$.

x	-2	-1	0	1	2	3
y						

(2 marks)

(b) Draw the graph of $y = 4x^2 - 4x - 3$ on the graph paper below.

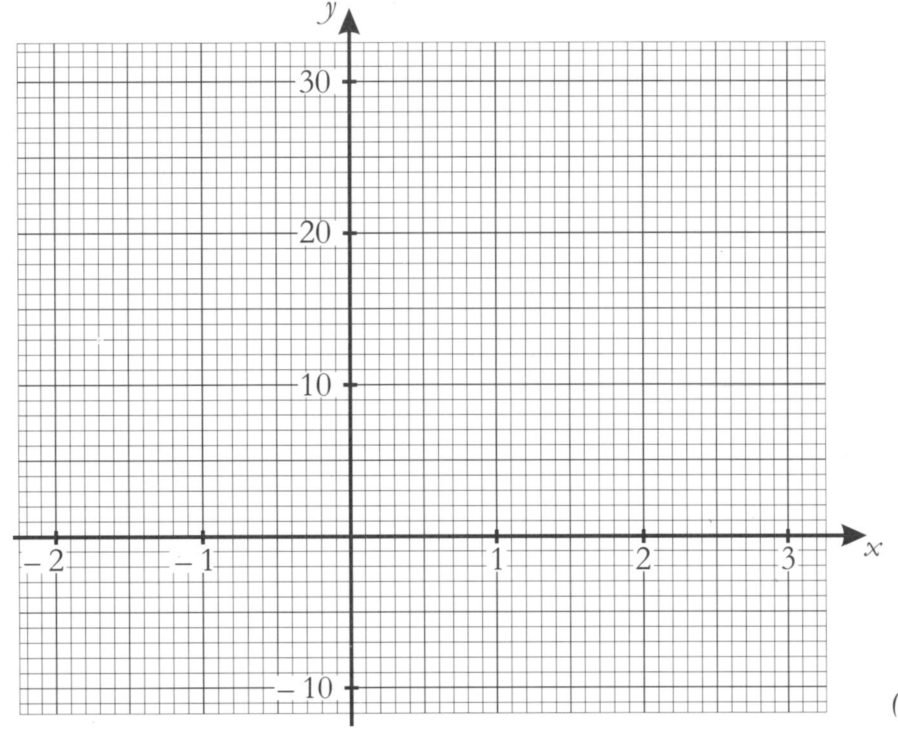

(2 marks)

(c) Solve $4x^2 - 4x - 3 = 0$, using your graph.

$x =$ .... or $x =$ .... *(2 marks)*

(d) Estimate the gradient of $y = 4x^2 - 4x - 3$ at the point where $x = -1$.

....

Answer .... *(3 marks)*

A60 **(a)** Complete the table of values for $y = x^2 - 2x - 1$.

x	-3	-2	-1	0	1	2	3
y							

(b) Draw the graph of $y = x^2 - 2x - 1$ on the graph paper below.

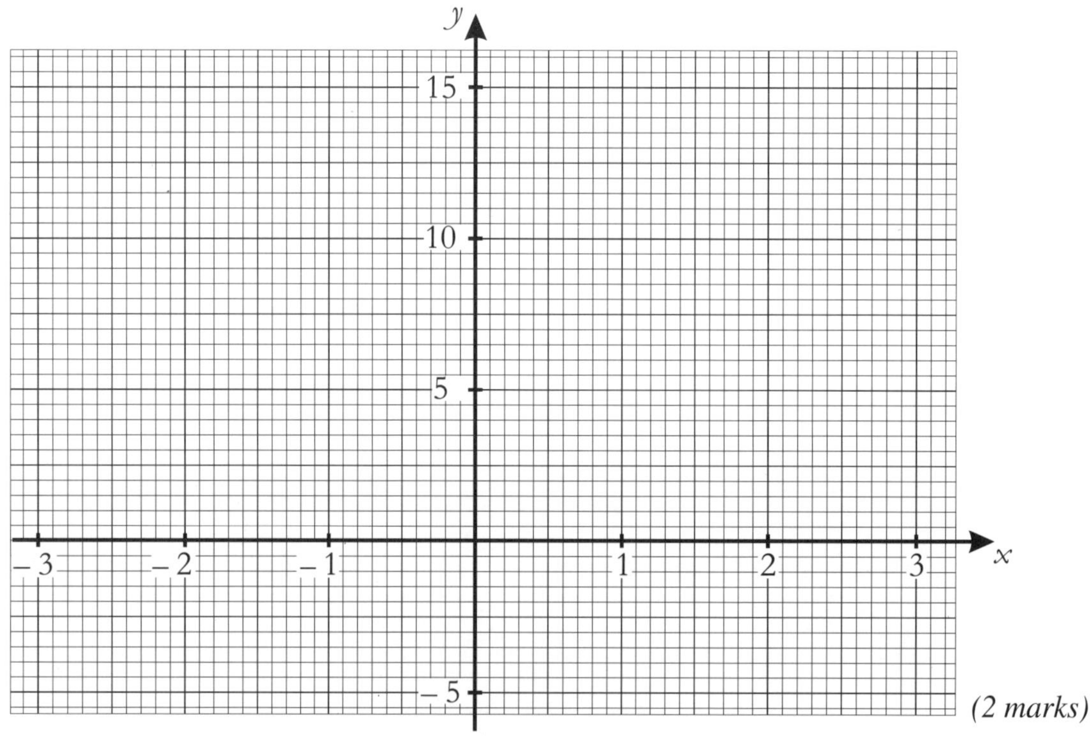

(2 marks)

(c) Solve $x^2 - 2x - 1 = 0$ using your graph.

$x =$ .... or $x =$ .... *(2 marks)*

(d) Estimate the gradient of $y = x^2 - 2x - 1$ at the point where $x = -2$.

....

Answer .... *(3 marks)*

A61 (a) Draw the graph of $y = x^3 + 1$ for values of x from -3 to 3.

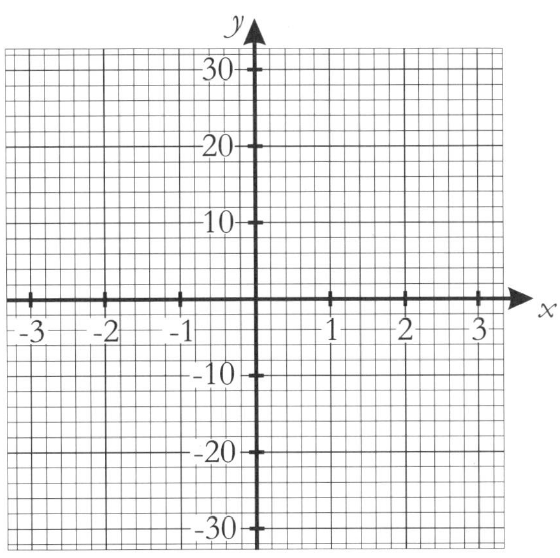

(3 marks)

(b) Use your graph to find the value of x where $y = 10$.

Answer x = ...*(1 mark)*

(c) Use your graph to solve $x^3 + 1 = 0$.

Answer x = ...*(1 mark)*

(d) Use your graph to solve $x^3 = 19$.

Answer x = ...*(1 mark)*

A62 (a) Draw the graph of $y = -x^3 + 2$ for values of x from -3 to 3.

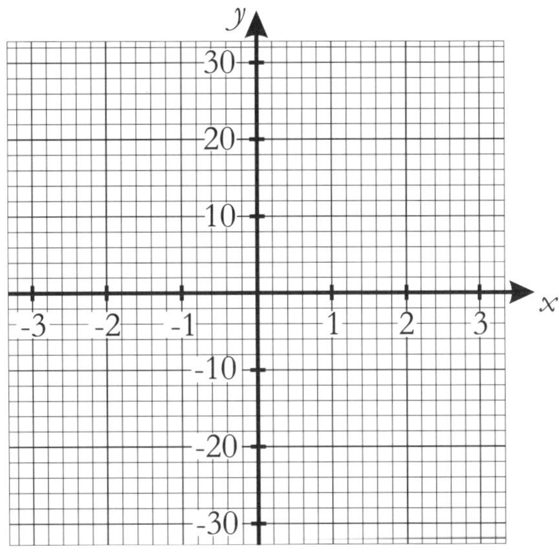

(3 marks)

Cubic Graphs

(b) Use your graph to find the value of x where $y = 20$.

Answer x = ...*(1 mark)*

(c) Use your graph to solve $-x^3 + 2 = 0$.

Answer x = ...*(1 mark)*

(d) Use your graph to solve $x^3 = 12$.

Answer x = ...*(1 mark)*

Travel Graphs & Speed

A63 I once ran the 400 m in 48.6 seconds.
What was my average speed in metres per second?

....

Answer .... m/s *(2 marks)*

A64 A car travelled 182 miles in 3.5 hours.
What was the average speed in miles per hour?

....

Answer .... mph *(2 marks)*

A65 How far would a train travelling at an average speed of 62 km/h travel in 90 minutes?

....

....

Answer .... km *(3 marks)*

A66 A man ran at an average speed of 3.2 m/s for 8 minutes.
How many kilometres did he travel?

....

....

Answer .... km *(3 marks)*

A67 Pippa and Sarah take part in an 80 m roller-blading race. Their progress is shown in the graph below.

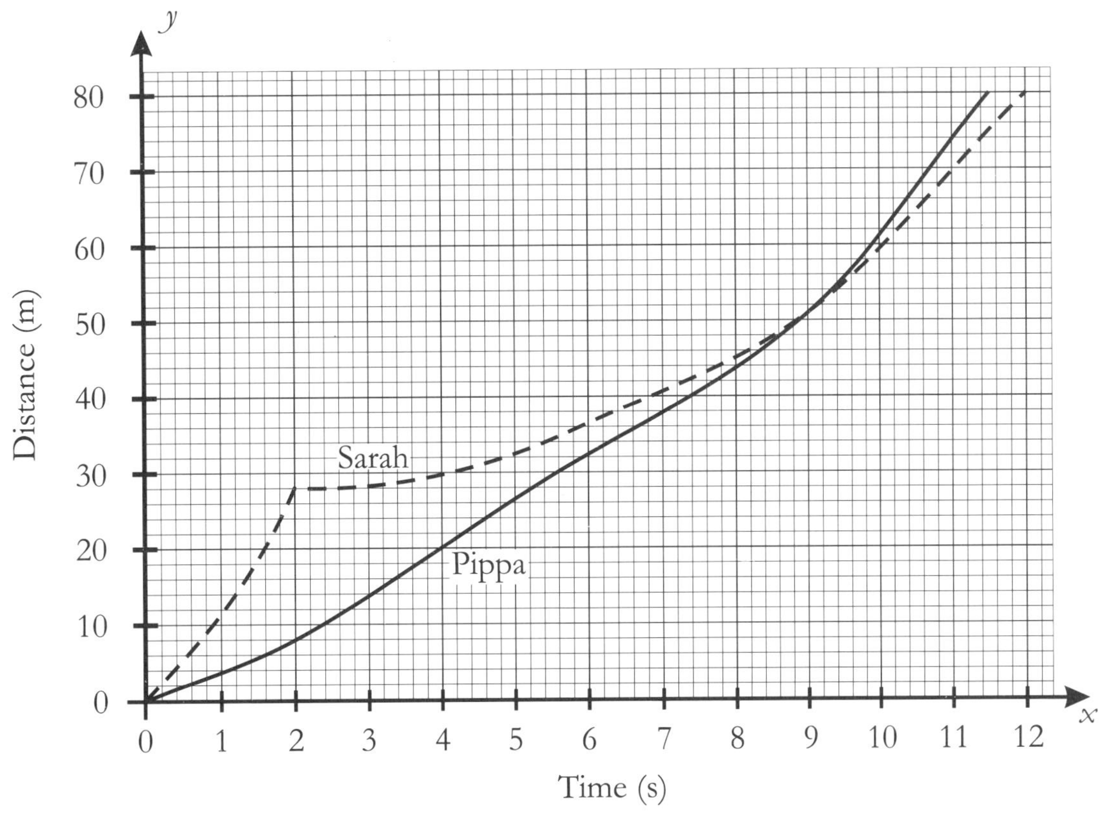

(a) Who won the race?

Answer ....*(1 mark)*

(b) What was the maximum distance between Pippa and Sarah during the race?

Answer ....m *(1 mark)*

(c) What happened to Sarah 2 seconds after the start of the race?

....

....*(1 mark)*

(d) Who was going the fastest at 9 seconds? Explain.

....

....*(1 mark)*

Travel Graphs & Speed

A68 This graph shows the speed of a motorcyclist during a short journey.

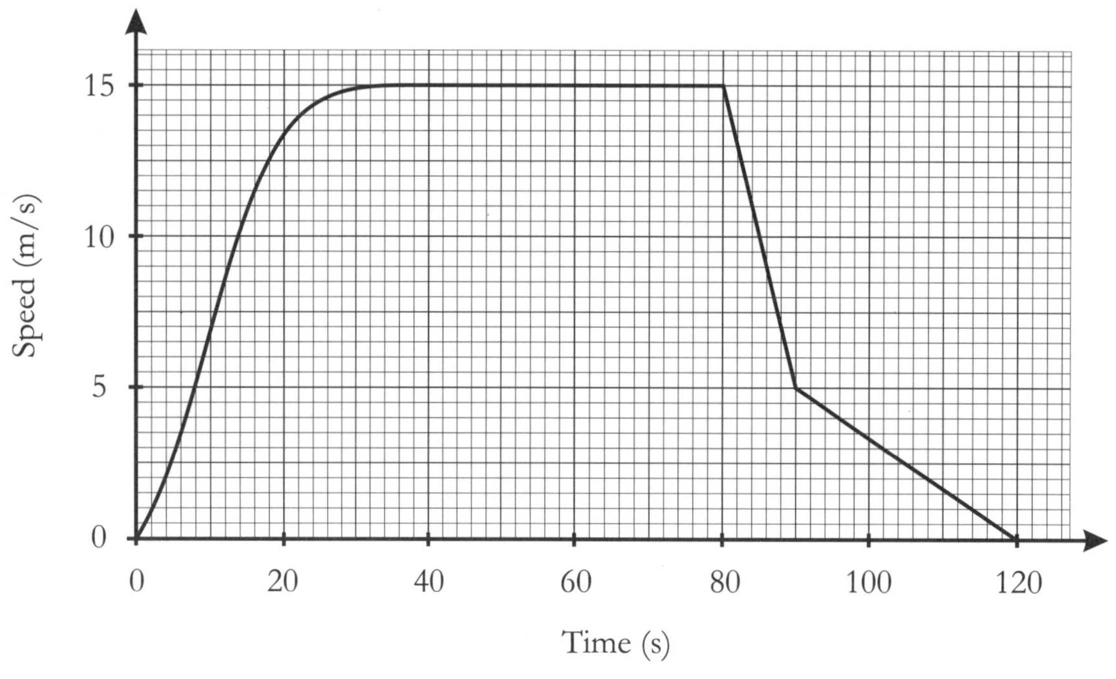

(a) How fast was the motorcyclist travelling after 90 seconds?

Answer .... m/s *(1 mark)*

(b) What was the acceleration of the motorcyclist after 20 seconds?

....

Answer .... m/s^2 *(3 marks)*

(c) Calculate an estimate for the total distance travelled by the motorcyclist during the journey.

....

....

....

....

Answer .... m *(3 marks)*

A69 The graph below shows how the speed of a train varies over its journey between two stations *A* and *C*.

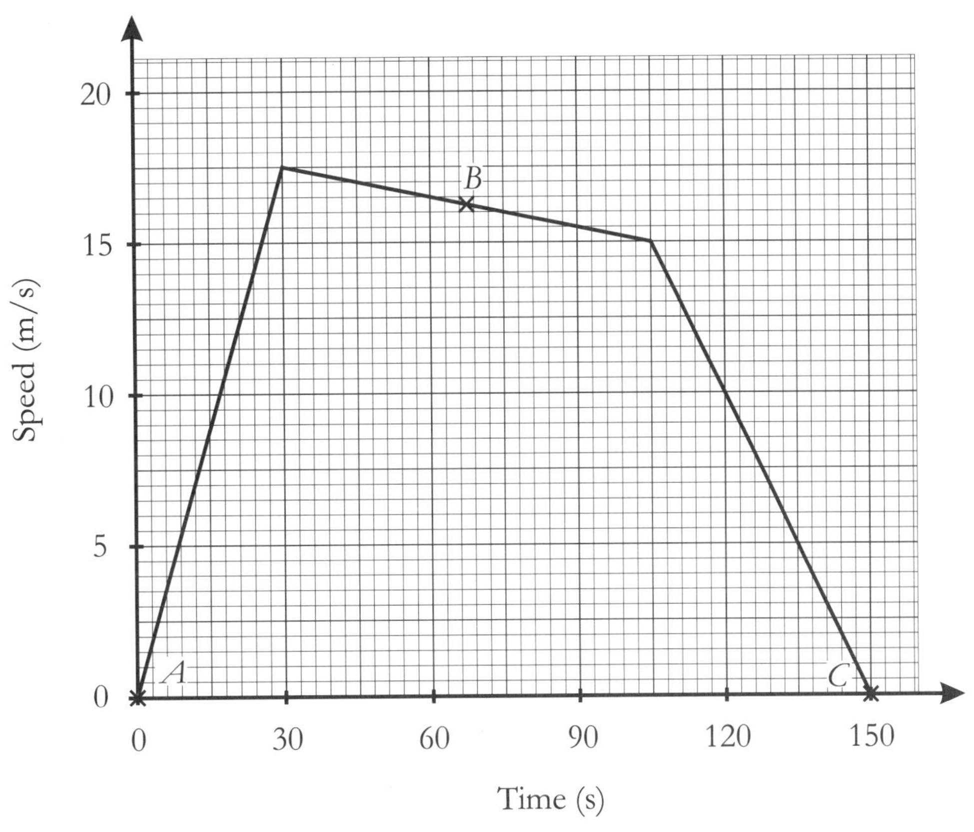

(a) What was the speed of the train at point *B*?

Answer .... m/s *(1 mark)*

(b) What was the acceleration of the train at point *B*?

....

Answer .... m/s² *(3 marks)*

(c) Using the graph, calculate the distance between the stations *A* and *C*.

....

....

....

....

Answer .... m *(3 marks)*

Algebra

Recognising & Transforming Graphs

A70 Label each graph with its equation.

A: $y = -x^2 + 2$ **B**: $y = \frac{1}{x}$ **C**: $y = -x^3$

D: $y = x + 2$ **E**: $y = x^2 - 2$ **F**: $y = x^3$

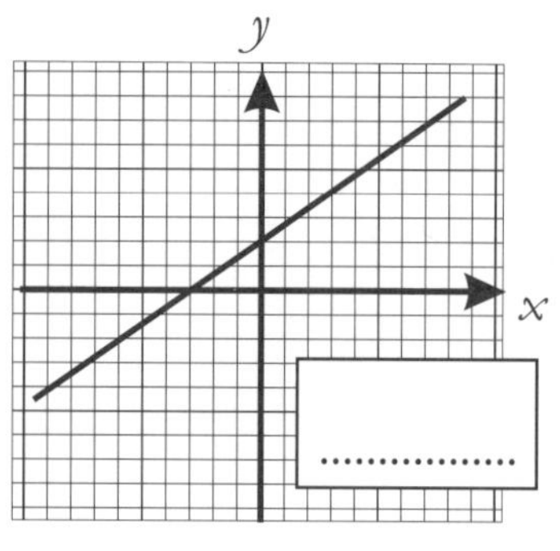

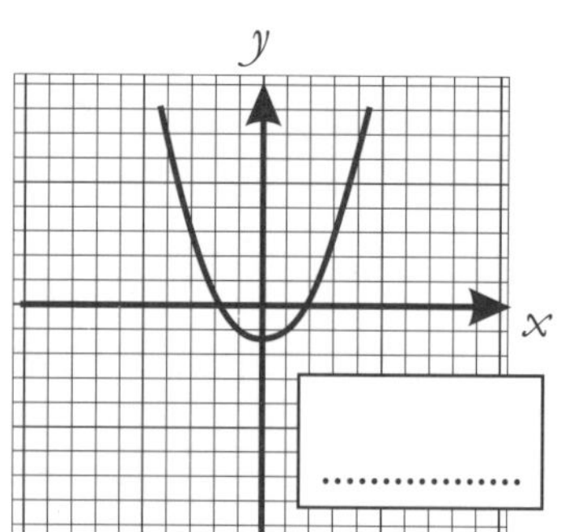

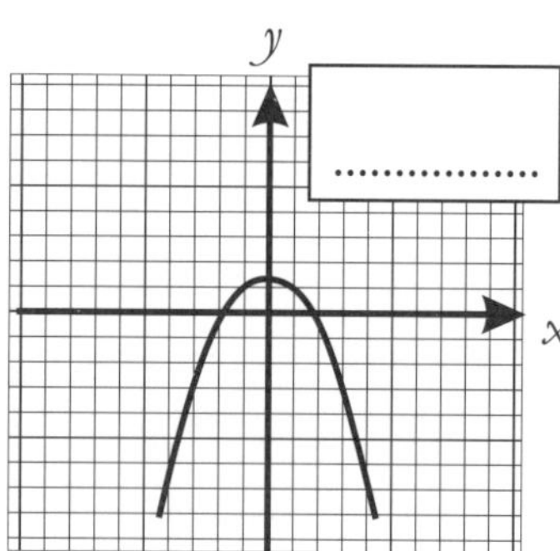

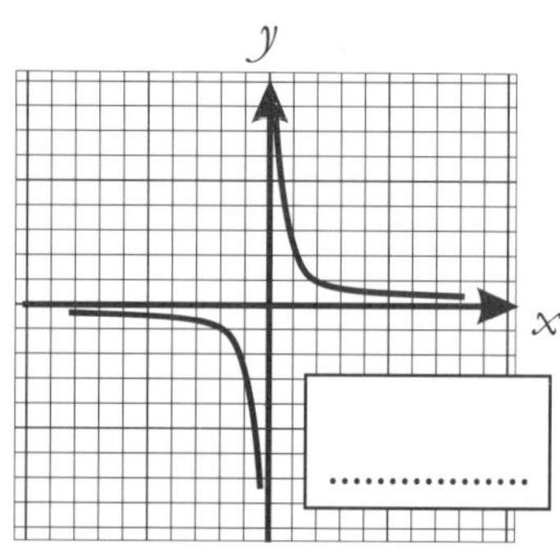

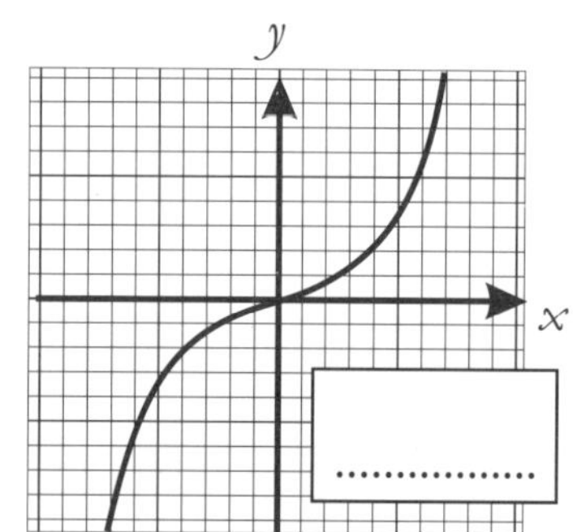

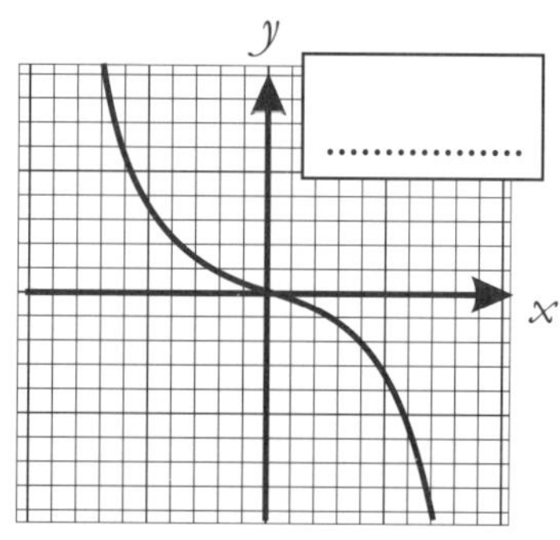

(3 marks)

A71 Which of these graphs cannot be $y = x^2 + 2$? Explain.

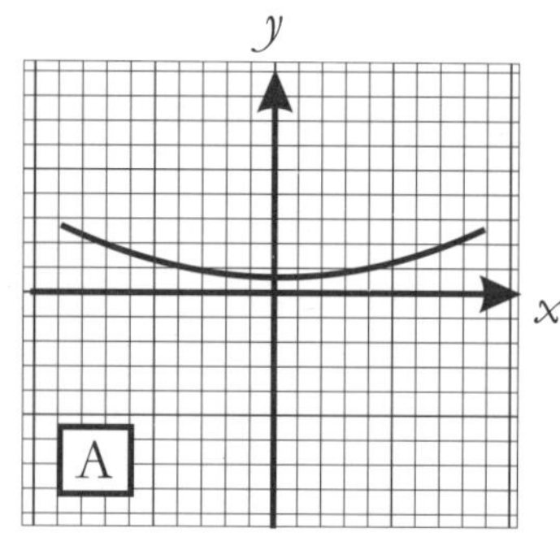

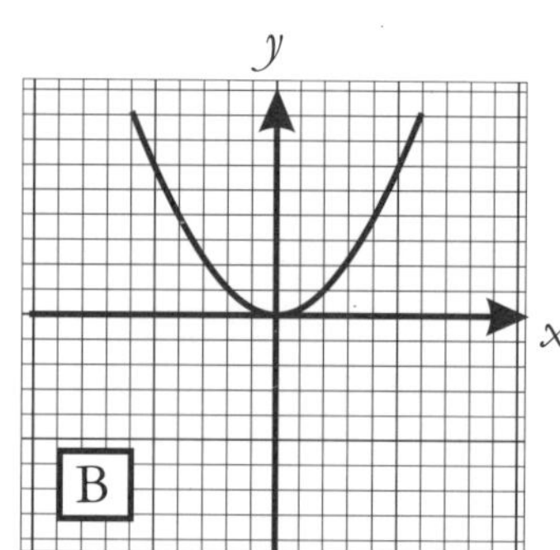

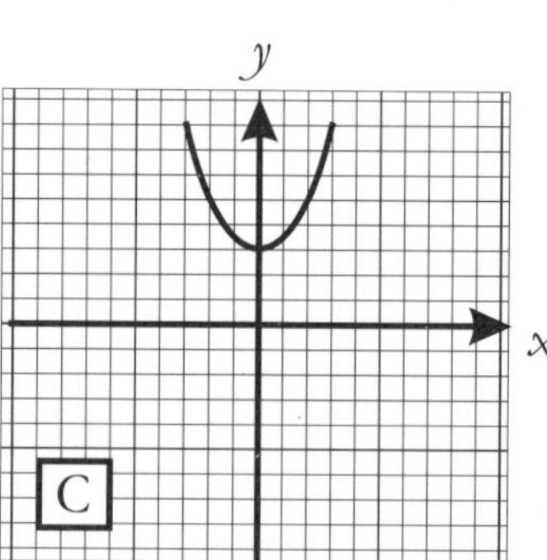

....

....

.... *(2 marks)*

A72 Water is poured into these odd-shaped vases at a constant rate.
Match each vase to the correct graph.

A *B* *D*

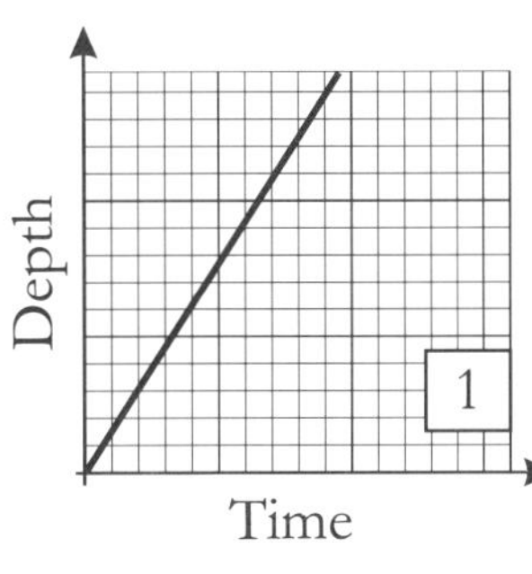

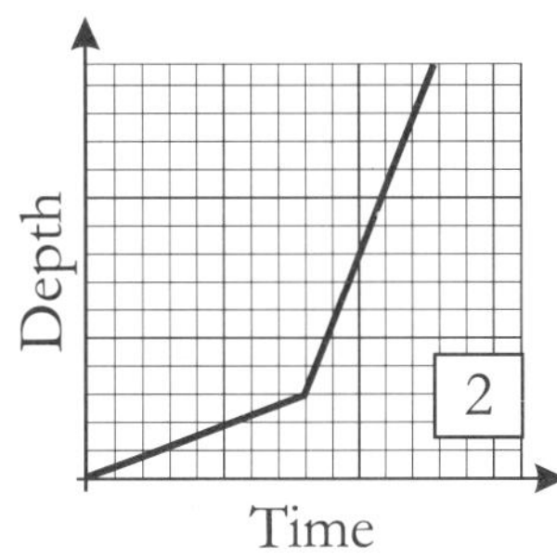

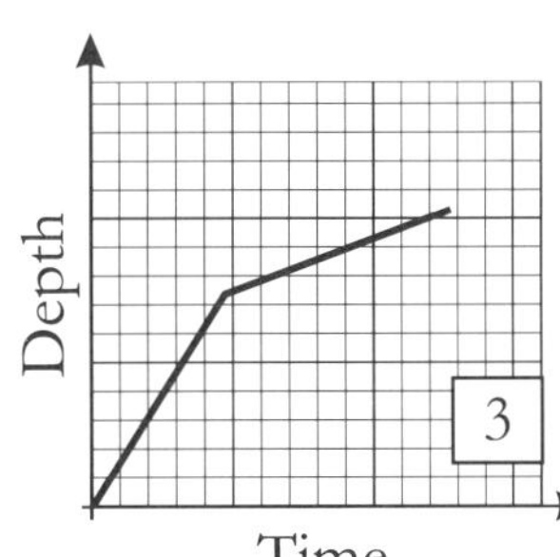

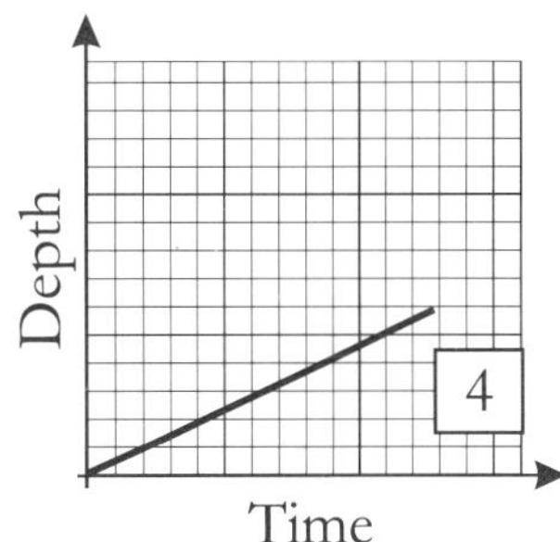

Vase *A* matches graph ....

Vase *B* matches graph ....

Vase *C* matches graph ....

Vase *D* matches graph .... *(2 marks)*

A73 Match the following graphs with the statements.

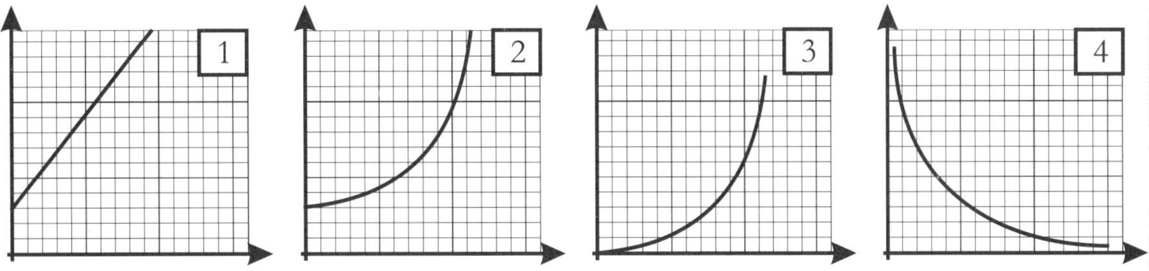

(a) The cost of hiring a taxi per mile including a fixed charge.

Graph ....

(b) $y = \frac{1}{x}$

Graph ....

(c) $y = x^3 + 4$

Graph ....

(d) The area of a circle as the radius increases.

Graph ....

(2 marks)

A74 The graph below is $y = f(x)$, where $f(x) = x^2 + x - 6$.

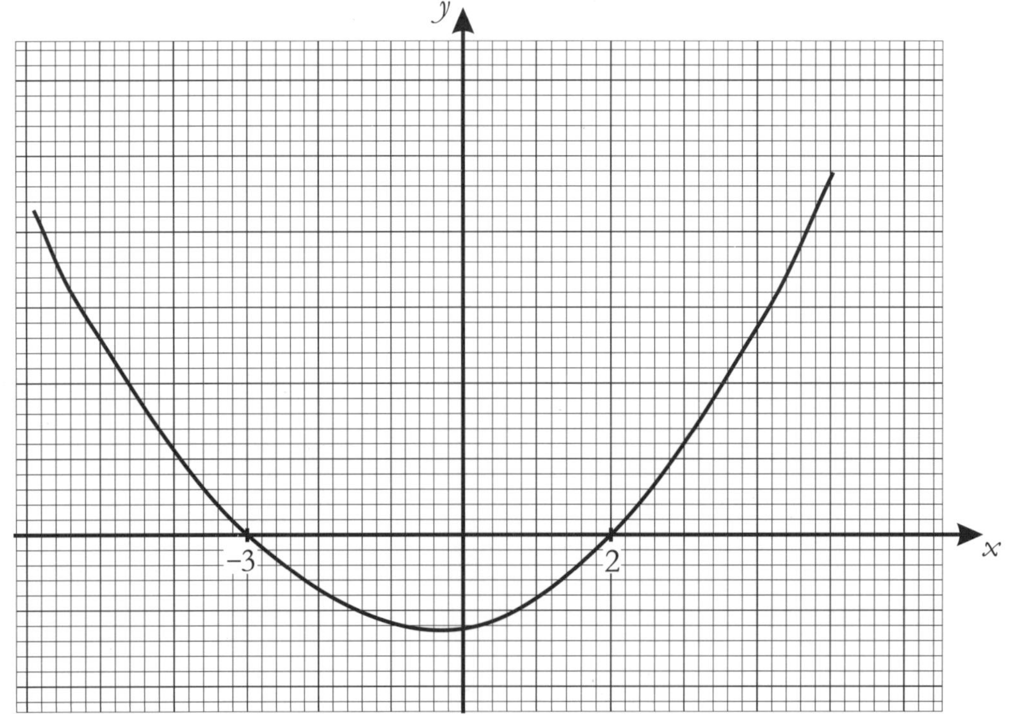

(a) Sketch $y = f(x - 2)$ on the same diagram, labelling the points where the curve cuts the x-axis.

(2 marks)

$y = f(x)$ crosses the y-axis at $y = -6$.

(b) Find the coordinates of the point where the graph of $y = 3f(x)$ crosses the y-axis.

....

....

Answer .... *(2 marks)*

A75 The graph below is $y = f(x)$, where $f(x) = x^3 + 4x^2 - 4x - 16$.

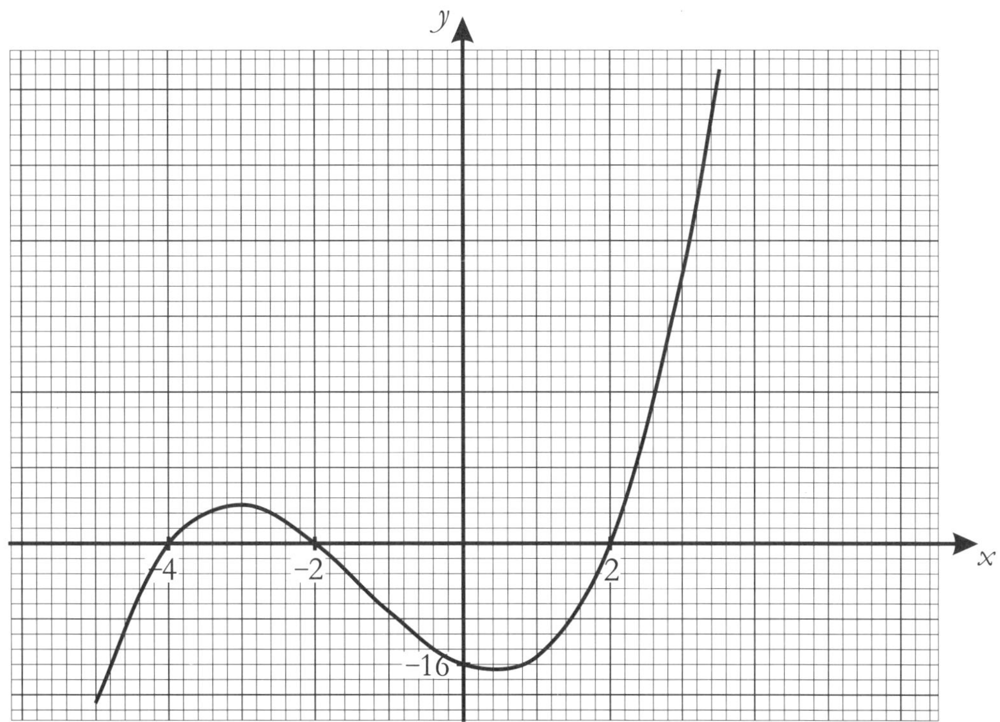

(a) Sketch the graph of $y = f(x) + 10$. Label where the graph cuts the y-axis.

(2 marks)

(b) The curve $y = f(x)$ is reflected in the y-axis. What is the equation of the new curve?

....

Answer $y =$ .... *(2 marks)*

Algebra

SEQUENCES

A76 $1 + (2 \times 3), 2 + (3 \times 4), 3 + (4 \times 5), \ldots$

The numbers above are the first 3 terms of a sequence.

(a) What is the fifth term?

....

Answer ....*(1 mark)*

(b) Work out the *n*th term, simplifying your answer.

....

....

Answer .... *(3 marks)*

A77

$(1 \times 2)^2, (2 \times 3)^2, (3 \times 4)^2, \ldots$

The numbers above are the first 3 terms of a sequence.

(a) What is the seventh term?

....

Answer ....*(1 mark)*

(b) Work out the *n*th term of the sequence and simplify your answer.

....

....

Answer .... *(3 marks)*

A78 The expression $\dfrac{n(n+4)(n-1)}{2}$ is the *n*th term for this sequence:

0, 6, 21, 48, ...

(a) Write down the *n*th term of the sequence below.

0, 12, 42, 96, ...

Answer ....*(1 mark)*

(b) Write down the *n*th term of the sequence below.

2, 8, 23, 50, ...

Answer ....*(1 mark)*

A79 $n^2(n-3)^2$ is the *n*th term of the sequence:

4, 4, 0, 16, ...

(a) What is the *n*th term of the sequence

2, 2, 0, 8, ... ?

Answer ....*(1 mark)*

(b) What is the *n*th term of the sequence

0, 0, -4, 12, ... ?

Answer ....*(1 mark)*

A80 For each of the sequences below, work out an algebraic expression for the *n*th term.

(a) 2, 7, 12, 17, 22, ...

....

....

....

Answer .... *(2 marks)*

(b) 3, 4, 6, 9, 13, ...

....

....

....

....

Answer .... *(3 marks)*

Algebra

Sequences

A81 Work out algebraic expressions for the nth terms of the sequences below.

(a) 3, 7, 11, 15, 19, ...

....

....

....

Answer .... *(2 marks)*

(b) 5, 7, 11, 17, 25, ...

....

....

....

....

Answer .... *(3 marks)*

Direct & Inverse Proportion

A82 **(a)** a is directly proportional to b. If $a = 8$ when $b = 6$, work out

(i) the value of a when $b = 10$,

....

....

Answer $a =$ .... *(2 marks)*

(ii) the value of b when $a = 66$.

....

....

Answer $b =$ .... *(1 mark)*

(b) Given that $x \propto \frac{1}{y^2}$, complete this table.

x	50		$\frac{1}{2}$	2
y	2	5		

(3 marks)

A83 (a) Given that $p \propto q^2$, complete this table.

p	80	180	5	
q	2			0

(3 marks)

(b) The time taken to paint a certain room is inversely proportional to the number of painters.
3 painters take 2 hours to paint the room.

(i) How long would 9 painters take to paint the room?

....

Answer .... minutes *(2 marks)*

(ii) If it takes 3 hours to paint the room, how many painters are there?

....

Answer .... painters *(1 mark)*

Volume & Area

S1 A triangular hole is punched out of a rectangular piece of card.

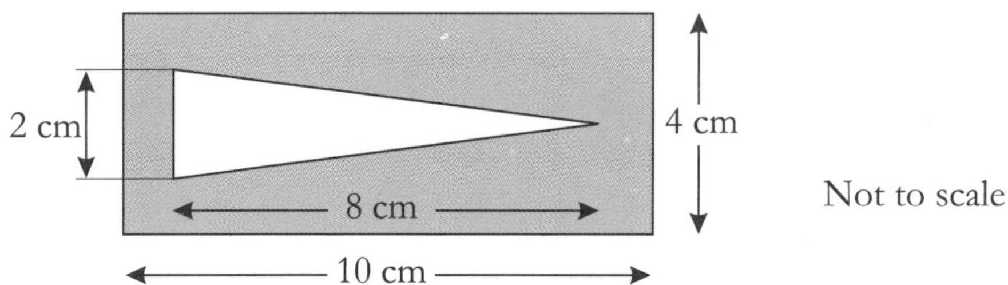

Work out the area of the remaining card.

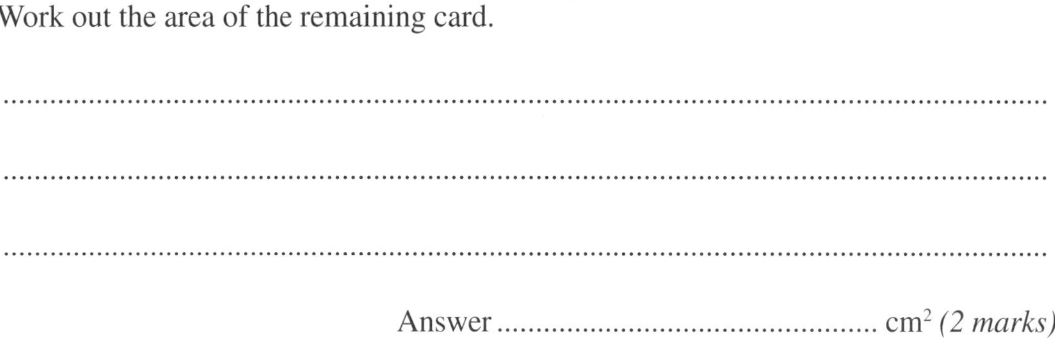

....

....

....

Answer .... cm^2 *(2 marks)*

S2 A kite shaped shield is cut from a rectangular piece of plastic.

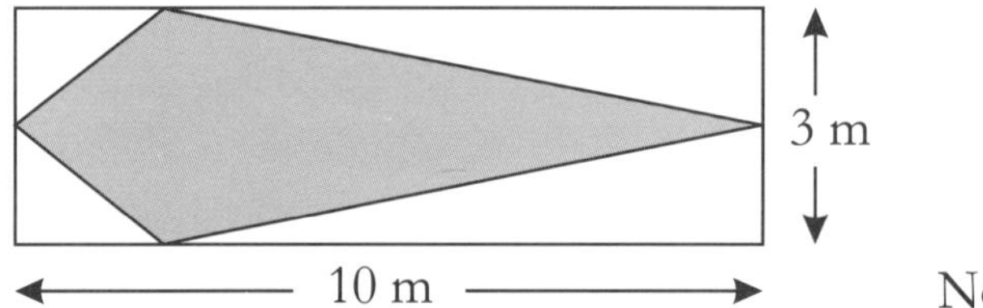

Not to scale

Calculate the area of the kite shaped shield.
State your units.

....

....

....

Answer .... *(3 marks)*

S3

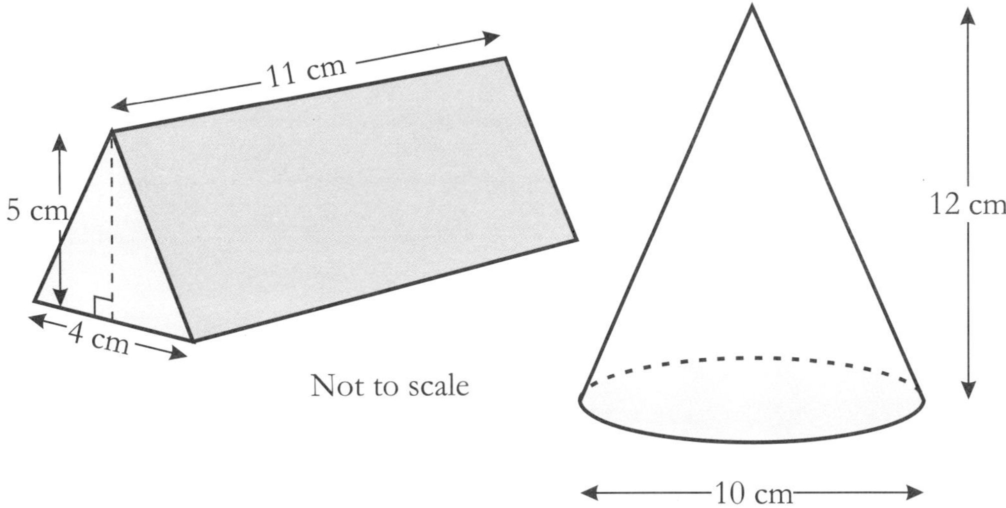

(a) Work out the difference in volume between the prism and the cone.
(The volume of a cone is $\frac{1}{3}\pi r^2 h$, where r is the base radius and h is the vertical height.)

....

....

....

....

....

Answer .... cm³ *(4 marks)*

(b) Work out the difference in the surface area of the prism and the surface area of the cone.
(The curved surface area of a cone is πrl, where l is the slant height.)

....

....

....

....

....

Answer .... cm² *(4 marks)*

Volume & Area

S4 The volume of a cylinder is 142.6 cm^3. The diameter of the base is 2.6 cm. Calculate, correct to 3 significant figures, the height of the cylinder.

....

....

Answer .... cm *(2 marks)*

S5 The triangular prism below has a volume of 132.9 cm^3. The length of the prism is 14.2 cm and the width is 3.1 cm.

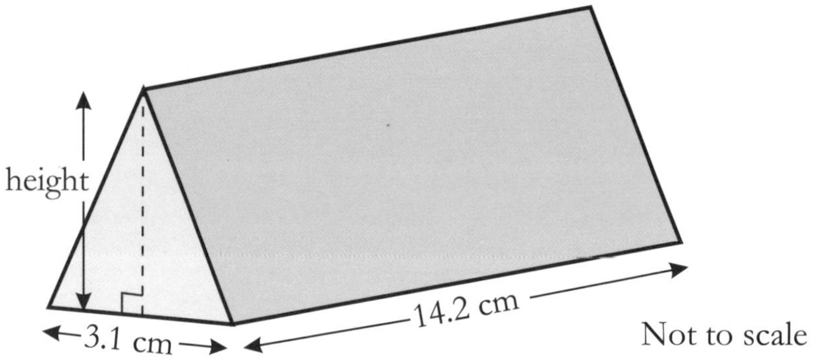

height

3.1 cm

14.2 cm

Not to scale

Calculate the height of the prism, correct to 1 decimal place.

....

....

....

Answer .... cm *(3 marks)*

S6 Calculate the volume of a sphere of radius 8 cm.

....

....

Answer .... cm^3 *(2 marks)*

S7 The surface area of a sphere is 3000 cm^2. Calculate the radius of the sphere.

....

....

Answer .... cm *(3 marks)*

S8 Steven thinks that the formula for the surface area of a certain solid is:

area = $\pi a^2 b$, where a and b are lengths.

Explain why Steven's formula is wrong.

....

.... *(1 mark)*

S9 **(a)** Which of the following formulae could be a volume?

A: $V = \pi r^2 + 4\pi h$
B: $V = r^3 + r^2 h + rh$
C: $V = \pi r^2 h^2$
D: $V = 4rh^2 + r^3$

Answer .... *(1 mark)*

(b) Explain your answer to **(a)**.

....

.... *(1 mark)*

S10

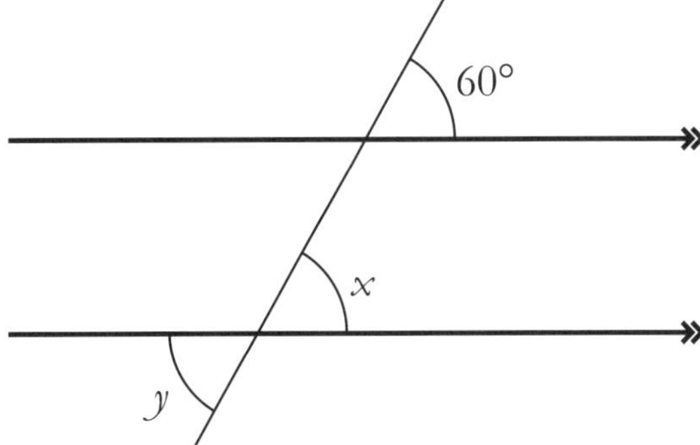

Not to scale

(a) Explain why angle x is 60°.

....

.... *(1 mark)*

(b) Write down the size of angle y.

Answer y = ... degrees *(1 mark)*

ANGLES

S11

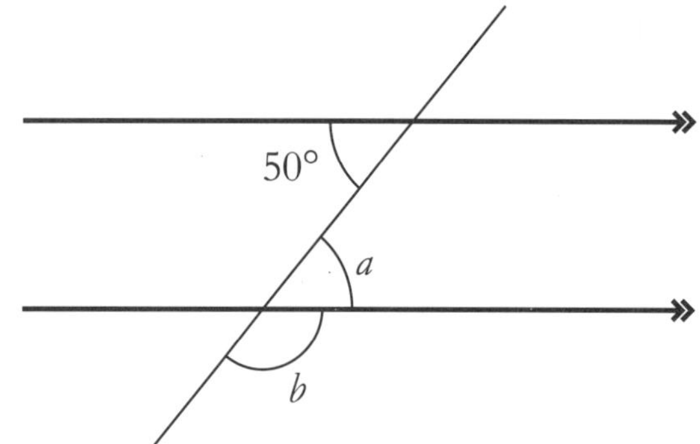

Not to scale

(a) Explain why angle a is 50°.

....

....*(1 mark)*

(b) What is the size of angle b?

....

Answer b = ... degrees *(1 mark)*

S12

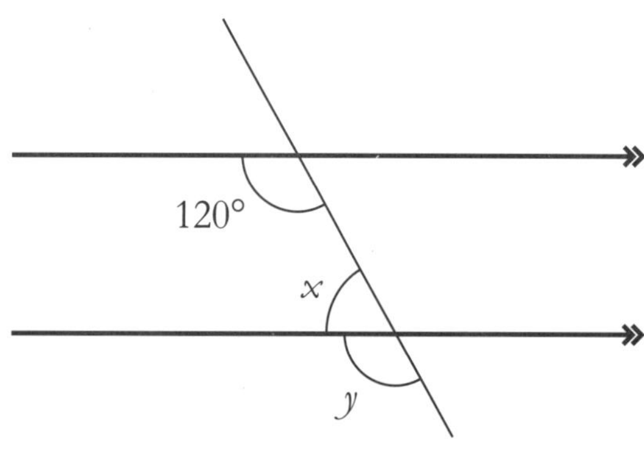

Not to scale

(a) Explain why angle x is 60°.

....

....*(1 mark)*

(b) What is the size of angle y?

....

Answer y = ... degrees *(1 mark)*

S13

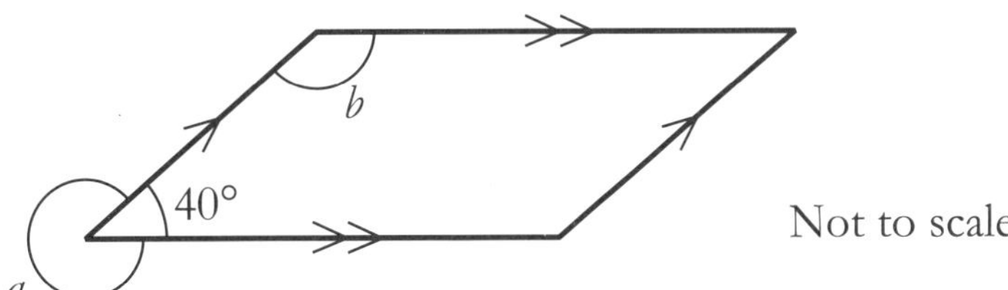

(a) Explain why angle a is 320°.

....

.... *(1 mark)*

(b) What is the size of angle b?

....

Answer b = ... degrees *(1 mark)*

S14 Work out the size of the angles marked $x°$.

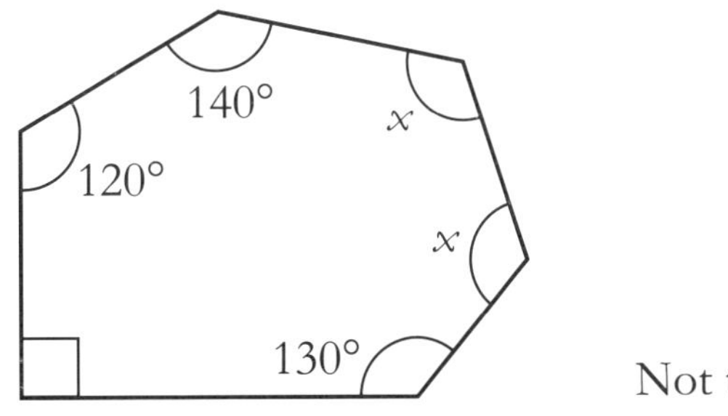

....

....

....

Answer x = ... degrees *(3 marks)*

ANGLES

S15 Using the diagram below, find the size of the angles marked x.

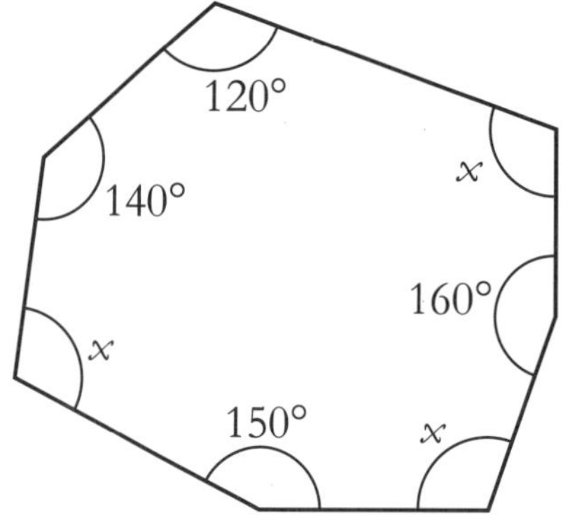

Not to scale

....

....

....

Answer x = ... degrees *(3 marks)*

S16 *WXYZ* is a quadrilateral. Angle *ZWX* = 80° and angle *WXY* = 100°.
Side *XY* is parallel to *WZ* and side *WX* is parallel to *YZ* .

(a) Draw a rough sketch of the quadrilateral *WXYZ*.

(3 marks)

(b) Write down the size of angle *XYZ*.

Answer .... degrees *(1 mark)*

S17 In the quadrilateral *ABCD*, angle *ABC* = 90°, angle *CDA* = 90°, angle *BCD* = 60° and *BC* = *CD*.

(a) Draw a rough sketch of the quadrilateral *ABCD*.

(3 marks)

(b) Find the size of angle *BAD*.

....

Answer .... degrees *(1 mark)*

S18 The diagram shows a circle of radius 5 cm with centre at *O*.
The angle at the centre of sector *AOB* is 30°.

Not to scale

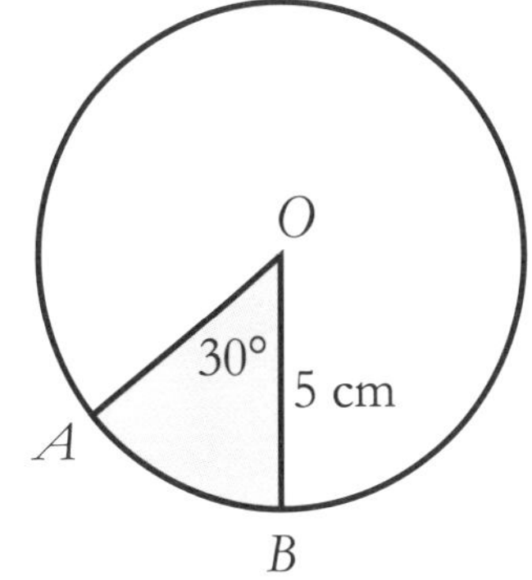

(a) What is the circumference of the circle?

....

....

Answer .... cm *(1 mark)*

arc AB?

....

....

Answer .... cm *(2 marks)*

aded sector, AOB?

....

....

Answer .... cm^2 *(2 marks)*

ircumscribed by a circle with centre O.
s 60 cm.

X
O
Z
Y

(a) Calculate the radius of the circle.

....

....

Answer .... cm *(2 marks)*

(b) Write down the size of angle XYZ.

Answer .... degrees *(1 mark)*

(c) Work out the area shaded.

....

....

....

Answer .... cm^2 *(3 marks)*

S20 Angle $AOC = 75°$, where O is the centre of the circle.
AP is a tangent to the circle.

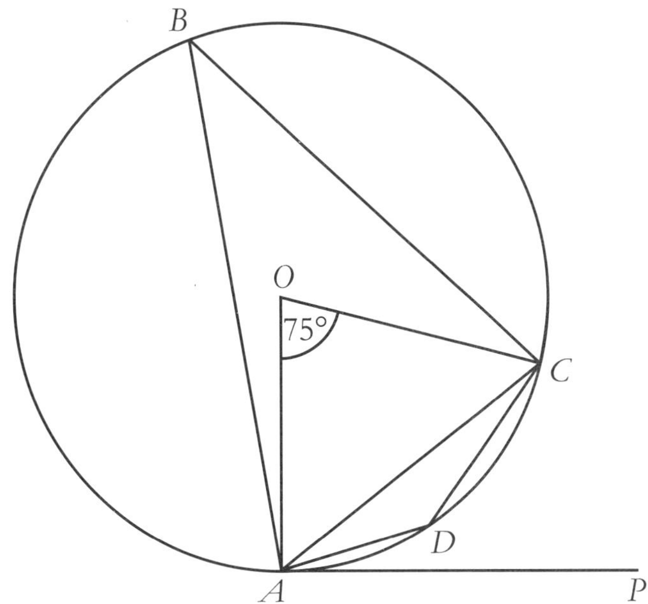

Not to scale

(a) Calculate the size of angle CAP.

....

....

....

Answer .... degrees *(2 marks)*

(b) Calculate the size of angle ADC.

....

....

....

Answer .... degrees *(2 marks)*

Circle Theorems

S21

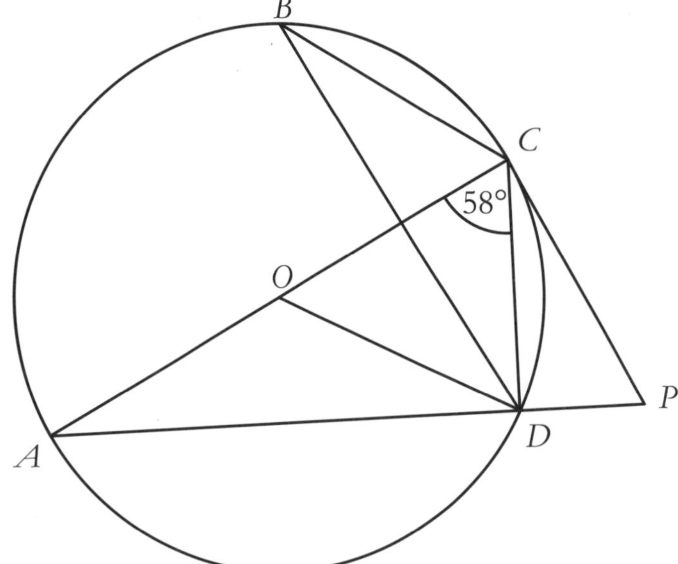

Not to scale

Angle $ACD = 58°$.
AC passes through the centre of the circle, O.
CP is a tangent to the circle and AP passes through D.

(a) Calculate the size of angle CBD.

....

....

....

Answer .... degrees *(2 marks)*

(b) Calculate the size of angle CPA.

....

....

....

Answer .... degrees *(2 marks)*

S22 Use Pythagoras' theorem to find the length AD.

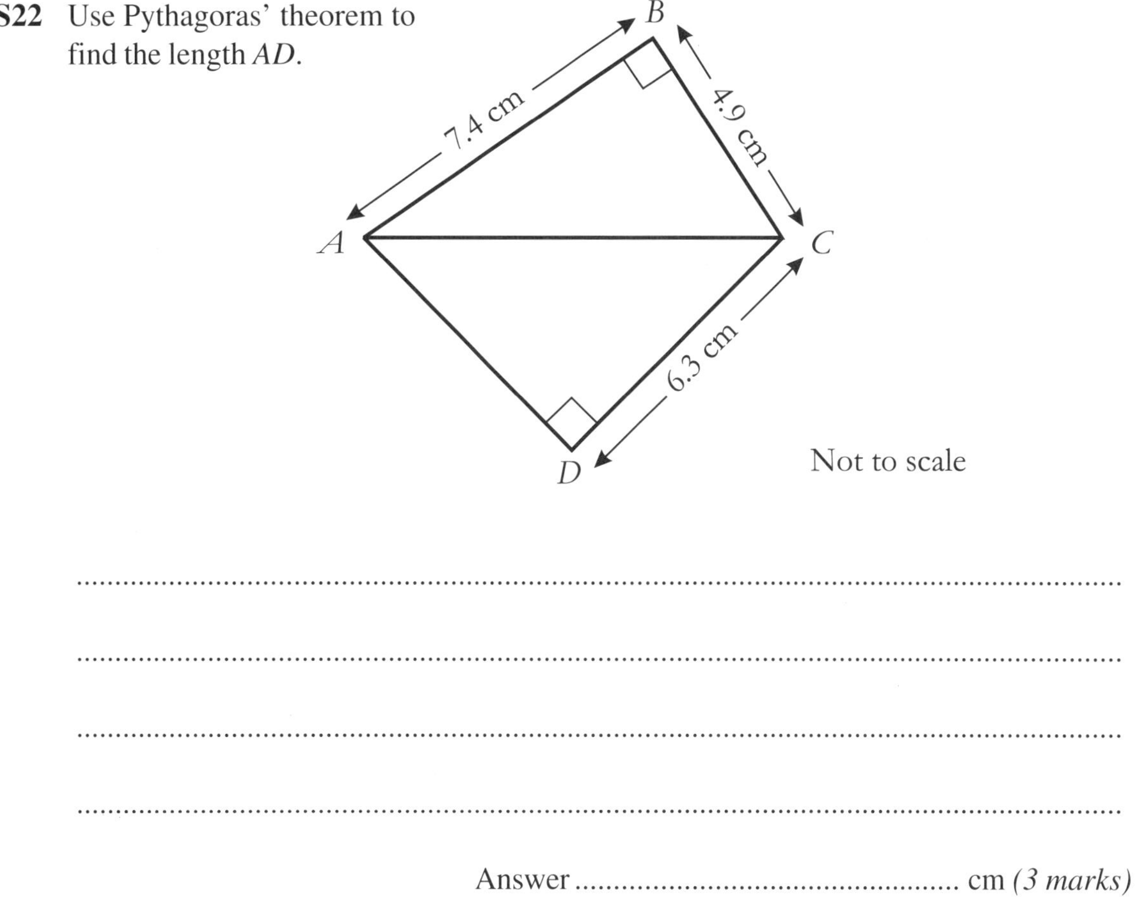

....

....

....

....

Answer .... cm *(3 marks)*

S23 Desmond runs 1500 m due east, then 800 m due north and then 600 m due west.
Calculate how far, in a straight line, Desmond is from his starting point.
It may be helpful to start by sketching a rough diagram.

Answer .... m *(3 marks)*

Trigonometry

S24

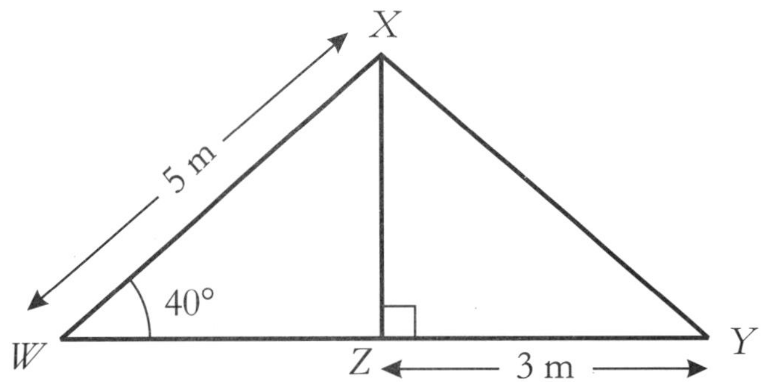

In the diagram above, $WX = 5$ m, $ZY = 3$ m and angle $XWZ = 40°$.
Calculate angle ZXY.

....

....

....

Answer $\angle ZXY =$ .... degrees *(3 marks)*

S25

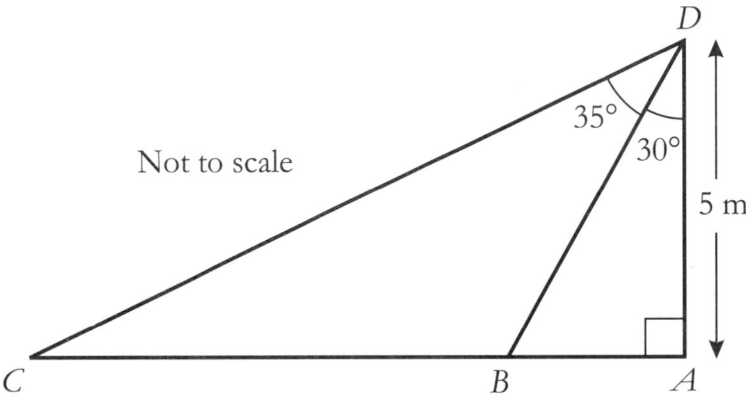

Length $AD = 5$ m, angle $ADB = 30°$ and angle $CDB = 35°$.
Calculate the length BC.

....

....

....

....

Answer .... m *(3 marks)*

S26 A tree *AB* is 15 m high. Point *C* is 52 m from *B*, the base of the tree, on level ground.

(a) Sketch a rough diagram to show this information.

(2 marks)

(b) What is the angle of elevation of *A* from *C*?

....

....

Answer .... degrees *(2 marks)*

S27 From a point *X*, Trevor walks 3 km south-west to point *Y* then 8 km south-east to point *Z*.

(a) Sketch a rough diagram to show Trevor's route.

(2 marks)

(b) Calculate the angle ZXY.

....

....

Answer .... degrees *(2 marks)*

(c) What is the size of angle XZY ?

....

Answer .... degrees *(1 mark)*

(d) Trevor walks back to X from Z in a straight line.
Calculate the distance XZ.

....

....

Answer .... km *(2 marks)*

S28 Length $WX = 40$ cm.
Calculate the length ZY.

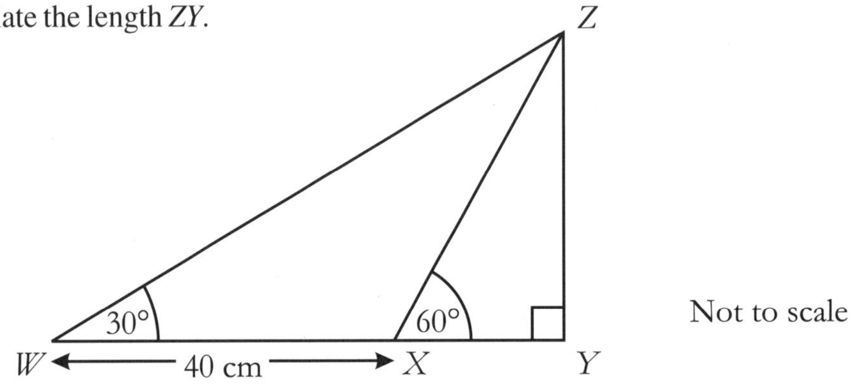

Z

30°

60°

W ← 40 cm → X

Y

Not to scale

....

....

....

....

Answer $ZY =$ .... cm *(5 marks)*

TRIGONOMETRY

S29

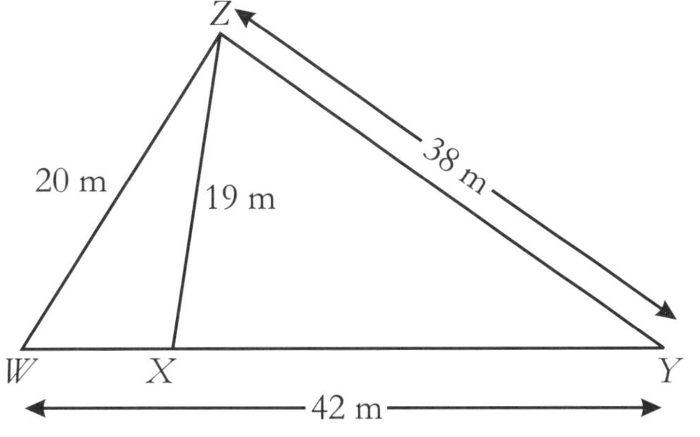

Not to scale

(a) Calculate the size of angle *WYZ*.

....

....

....

Answer .... degrees *(3 marks)*

(b) Calculate the size of angle *YXZ*.

....

....

Answer .... degrees *(2 marks)*

3D TRIGONOMETRY & PYTHAGORAS' THEOREM

S30 In this square-based pyramid,
E is vertically above *F*,
the midpoint of *AC*.
AB = 20 cm and *EC* = 40 cm.

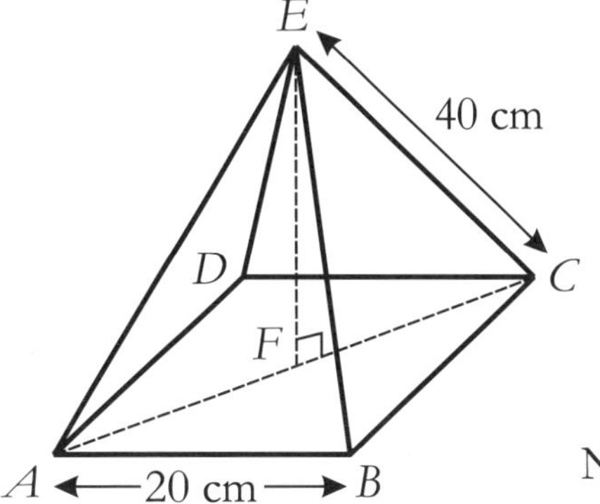

Not to scale

(a) Calculate the length *AF*.

....

....

Answer .... cm *(2 marks)*

(b) Find the angle between *EC* and the base *ABCD*.

....

....

Answer .... degrees *(2 marks)*

(c) Calculate the height of the pyramid *EF*.

....

....

Answer .... cm *(2 marks)*

S31 In this triangular prism,
F is vertically above *G*,
the midpoint of *AB*.
$AB = 4$ cm and $BC = 10$ cm.

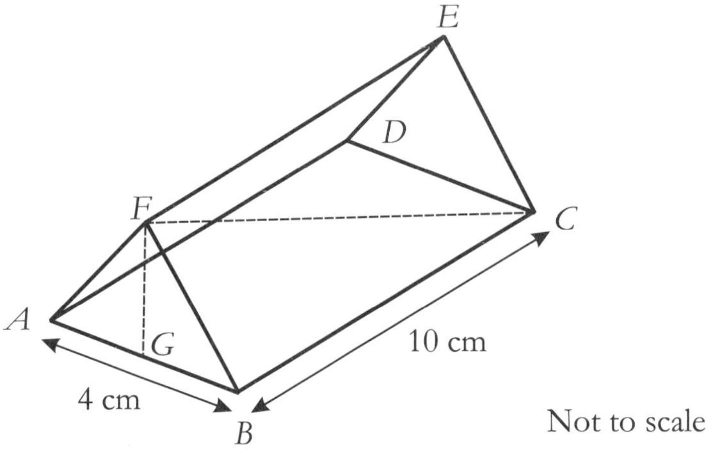

E
D
F
C
A
G
10 cm
4 cm
B

Not to scale

(a) Given that angle $AFB = 40°$, write down the size of angle *FAB*.

Answer .... degrees *(1 mark)*

(b) Work out the height of the triangular prism, *FG*.

....

....

Answer .... cm *(2 marks)*

(c) Work out the length *FC*.

....

....

Answer .... cm *(2 marks)*

S32

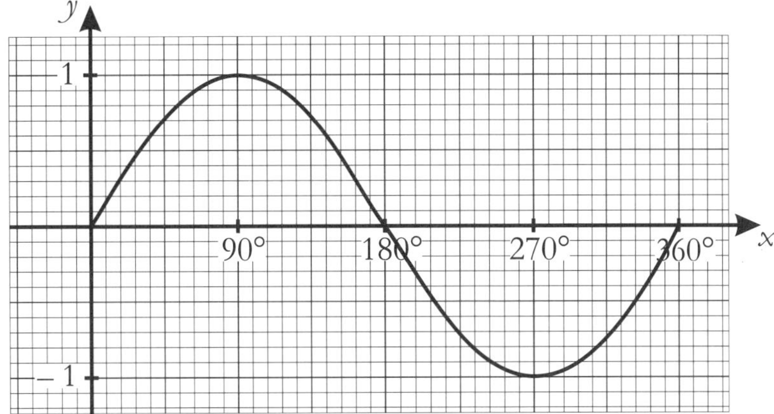

The graph shows $y = \sin(x)$, $0° \leqslant x \leqslant 360°$.

(a) Clearly show on the graph how you would find solutions to $\sin(x) = -0.5$ for $0° \leqslant x \leqslant 360°$.

(1 mark)

(b) Use your calculator to work out these solutions.

....

....

Answer x = ... *(2 marks)*

S33

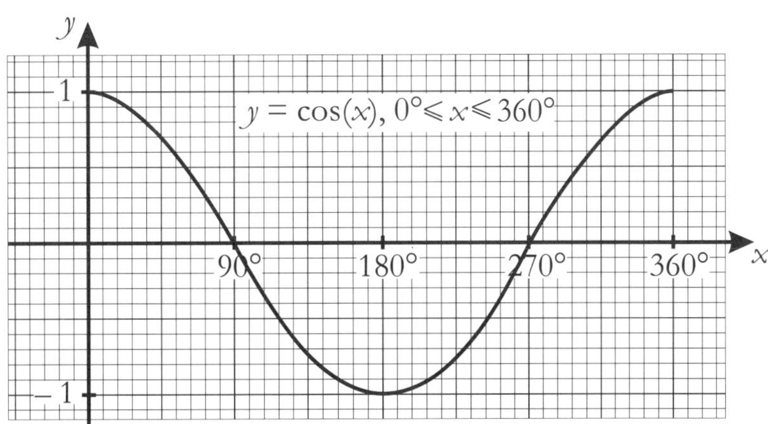

Use your calculator and the graph to find all the solutions of $\cos(x) = 0.2$, for values of x between 0° and 360°. Give your answers correct to 2 d.p.

....

....

....

Answer x = ... *(3 marks)*

Graphs of Trigonometric Functions

S34 **(a)** Without drawing a table of values, sketch the graph of $y = \tan(2x)$ for values of x from -180° to 180°.

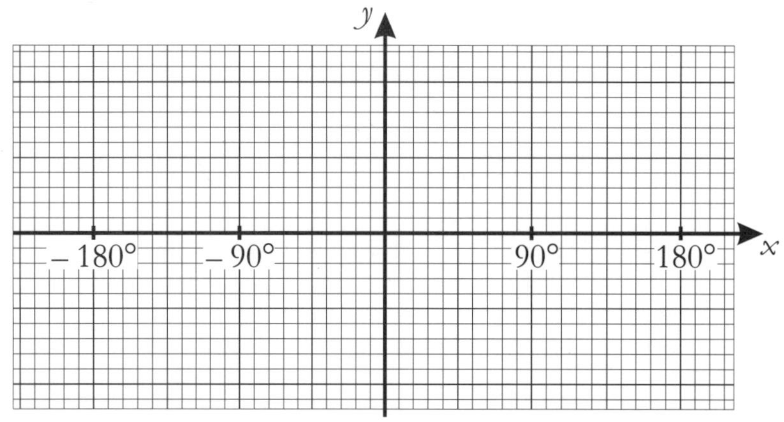

(b) Using your graph, find all the solutions to $\tan(2x) = 0$ for values of x between -180° and 180° inclusive.

Answer x = ... *(3 marks)*

Similar Shapes

S35

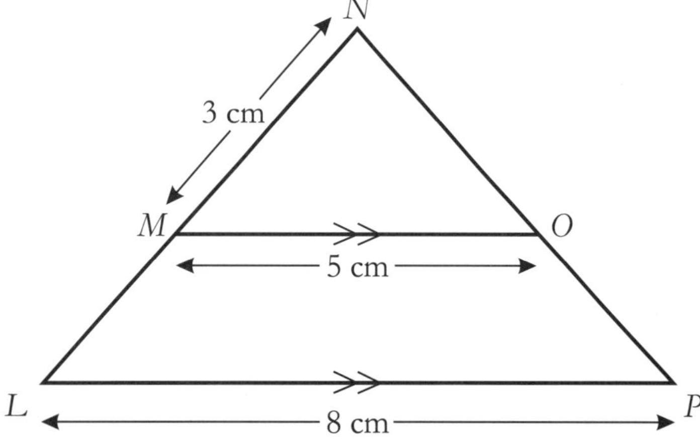

Not to scale

LP = 8 cm, MO = 5 cm, MN = 3 cm and LP is parallel to MO.
Calculate the length LN.

....

....

....

Answer .... cm *(2 marks)*

S36

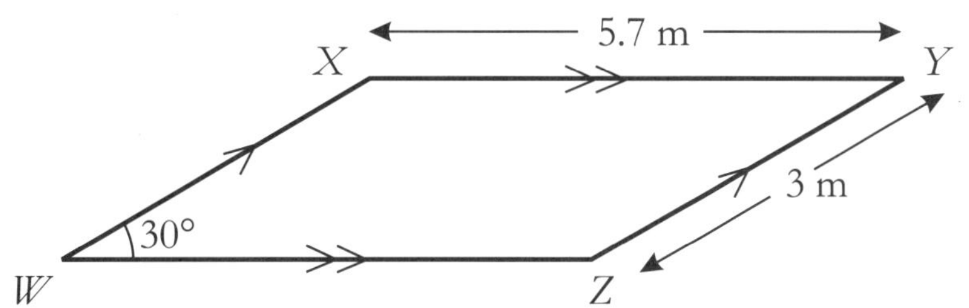

Not to scale

The parallelogram above is enlarged so that XY becomes 8.2 m.

(a) Calculate the new length of the side ZY.

....

....

Answer .... m *(2 marks)*

(b) What is the size of angle WXY in the enlarged parallelogram?

Answer .... degrees *(1 mark)*

S37 $\mathbf{a} = \begin{pmatrix} 4 \\ 3 \end{pmatrix}$, $\mathbf{b} = \begin{pmatrix} 2 \\ -1 \end{pmatrix}$

(a) Work out, as a column vector, $\mathbf{a} + \mathbf{b}$.

....

Answer ....*(1 mark)*

(b) What is $2\mathbf{a} - \mathbf{b}$?

....

Answer ....*(1 mark)*

Vectors

S38 $\mathbf{x} = \begin{pmatrix} -2 \\ -1 \end{pmatrix}$, $\mathbf{y} = \begin{pmatrix} 3 \\ -4 \end{pmatrix}$

(a) Work out, as a column vector, $\mathbf{x} - \mathbf{y}$.

....

Answer ....*(1 mark)*

(b) What is $2\mathbf{y} - 3\mathbf{x}$?

....

Answer ....*(1 mark)*

S39

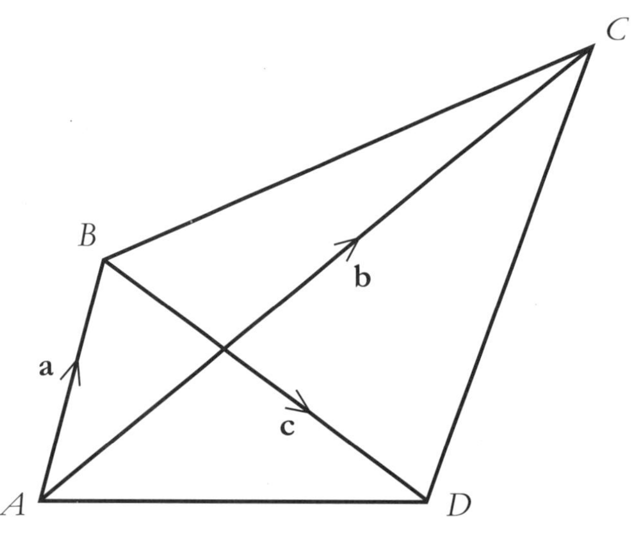

Not to scale

$\overrightarrow{AB} = \mathbf{a}$, $\overrightarrow{AC} = \mathbf{b}$, $\overrightarrow{BD} = \mathbf{c}$ and *ABCD* is a quadrilateral.

(a) Write down, in terms of **a**, **b** and **c**, the vectors

(i) $\overrightarrow{AD}$

Answer ....*(1 mark)*

(ii) $\overrightarrow{CB}$

Answer ....*(1 mark)*

(b) Given that $\overrightarrow{DC} = 2\mathbf{a}$, find an expression for $\mathbf{a}$ in terms of $\mathbf{b}$ and $\mathbf{c}$.

....

....

Answer $\mathbf{a}$ = ... *(2 marks)*

S40

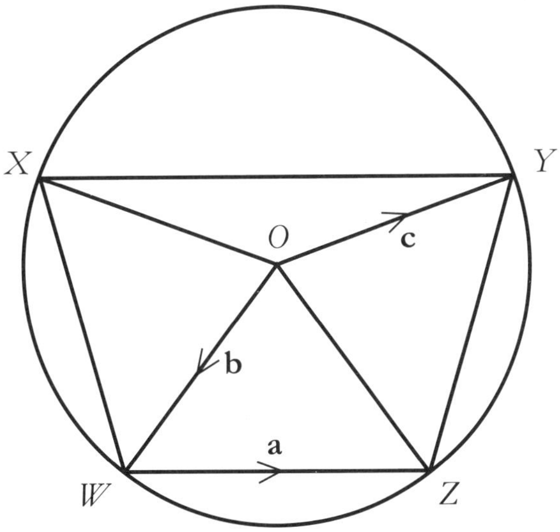

Not to scale

WXYZ is a cyclic quadrilateral, with *O* the centre of the circle.
$\overrightarrow{WZ} = \mathbf{a}$, $\overrightarrow{OW} = \mathbf{b}$ and $\overrightarrow{OY} = \mathbf{c}$.

(a) Find, in terms of $\mathbf{a}$, $\mathbf{b}$ and $\mathbf{c}$:

(i) $\overrightarrow{OZ}$

Answer ....*(1 mark)*

(ii) $\overrightarrow{ZY}$

Answer ....*(1 mark)*

(b) Given that the chord *XY* is twice as long and parallel to the chord *WZ*, find an expression for *XW* in terms of $\mathbf{a}$, $\mathbf{b}$ and $\mathbf{c}$.

....

....

Answer .... *(2 marks)*

TRANSFORMATIONS

S41 The diagram shows the position of three shapes, L, M and N.

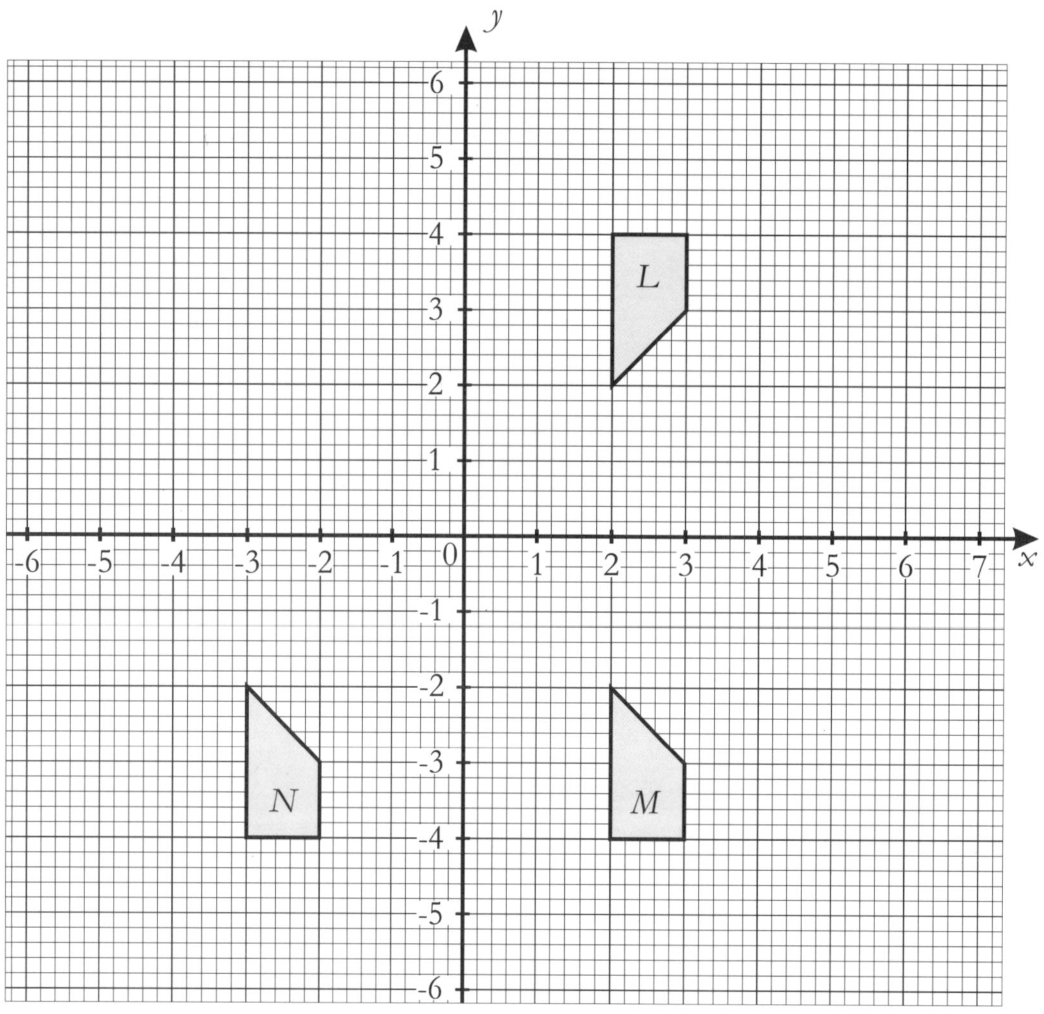

(a) Describe the transformation that moves L onto M.

....

....*(1 mark)*

(b) Describe the transformation that moves M onto N.

....

....*(1 mark)*

S42 The diagram shows the position of three shapes *A*, *B* and *C*.

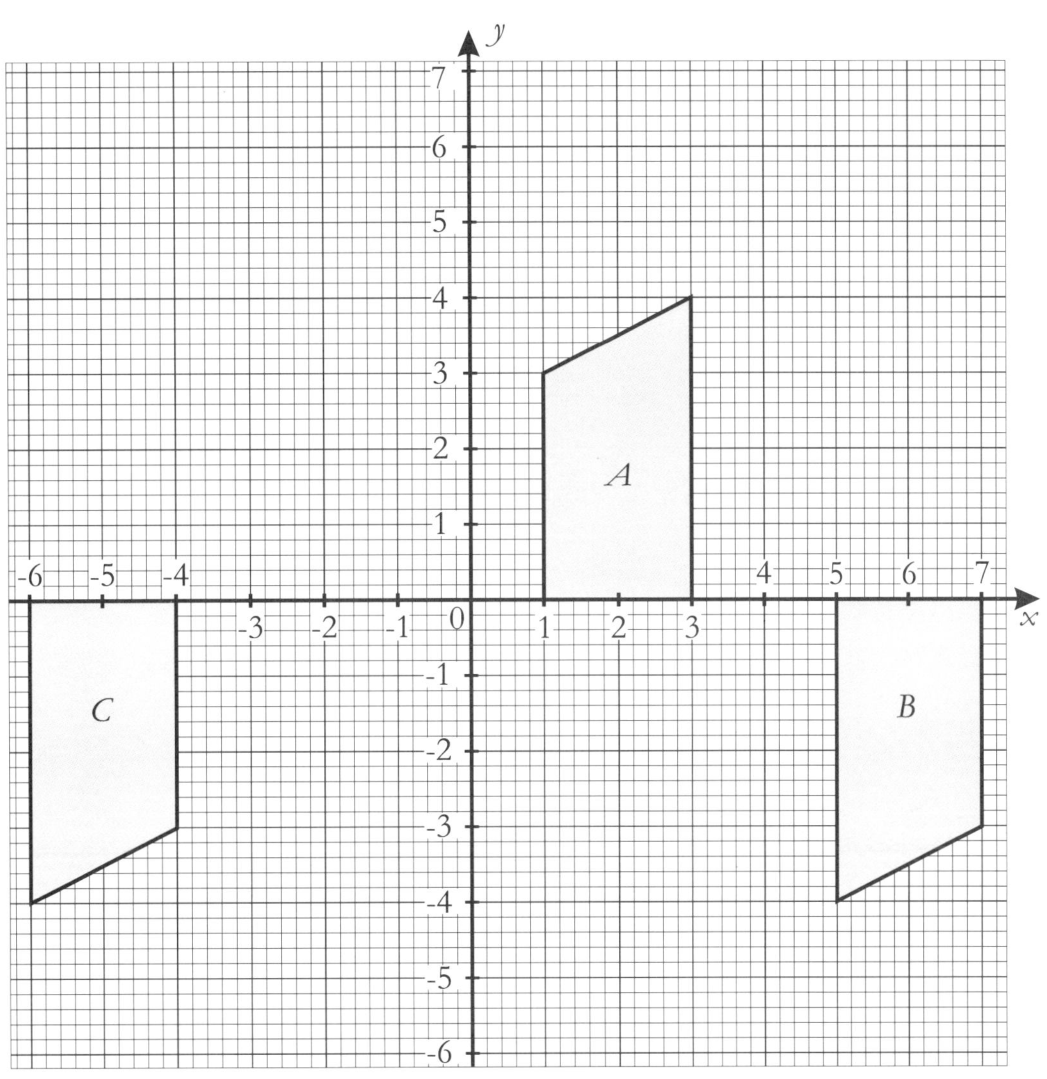

(a) Describe a single transformation that takes *A* onto *B*.

....

.... *(1 mark)*

Shape *A* is reflected in the *y*-axis.

(b) Draw the new position of *A*. Label it *D*. *(1 mark)*

(c) Describe a sequence of transformations which take *D* onto *C*.

....

.... *(2 marks)*

TRANSFORMATIONS

S43

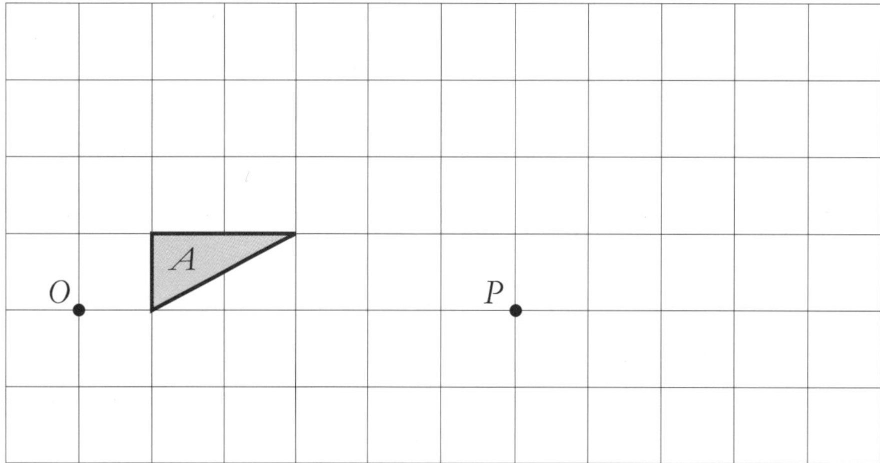

(a) Enlarge triangle A by a scale factor of 3 with centre of enlargement O. Label the enlarged triangle B. *(2 marks)*

(b) Draw an enlargement of triangle B with a scale factor of $-\frac{1}{3}$ and centre P. *(2 marks)*

S44 Shape A is enlarged to obtain shape B.

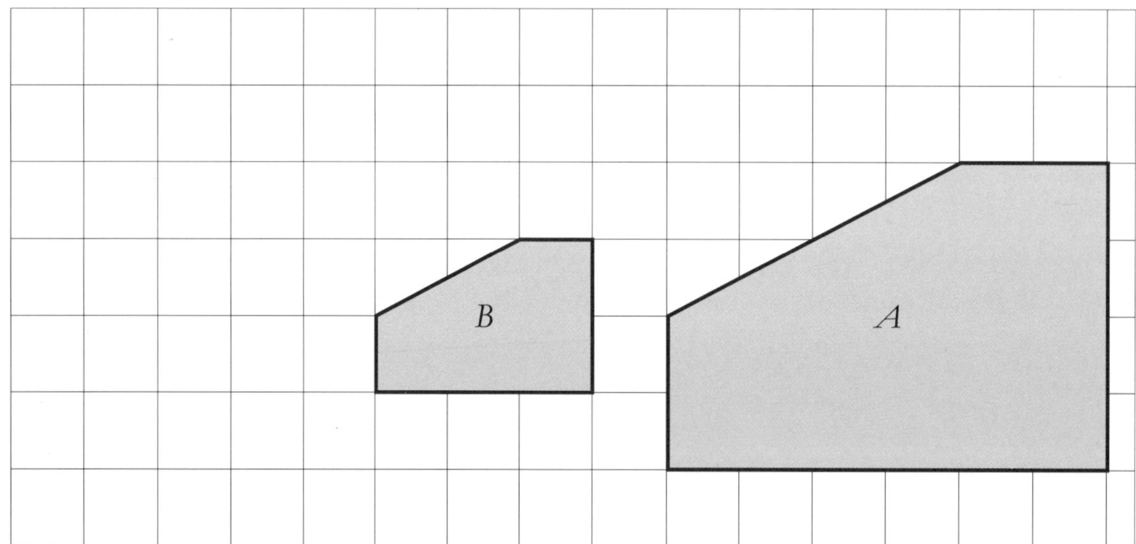

(a) What is the scale factor of the enlargement?

....

Answer .... *(1 mark)*

(b) Mark with a cross the centre of enlargement for the transformation. *(1 mark)*

S45 Below is a map of an island.

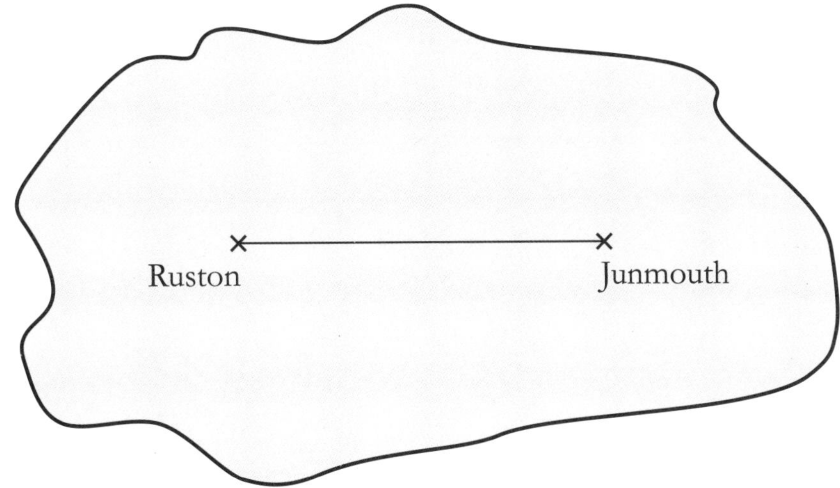

The scale of the map is 1:40 000.

(a) What is the distance between Ruston and Junmouth in metres?

....

Answer .... m *(2 marks)*

Marham is on a bearing of 030° from Ruston and a bearing of 300° from Junmouth.

(b) Mark on the map the position of Marham. *(2 marks)*

Bearings & Loci

S46 Below is a scale drawing of two boats at sea.
Boat Q is due south of boat P.

× P

× Q

The scale of the drawing is 1:10 000.

(a) How far in real life is boat P from boat Q?

....

....

Answer .... m *(2 marks)*

(b) Mark on the diagram the position of boat R, which is 1000 m from P on a bearing of 120°.

....

.... *(2 marks)*

S47 The diagram shows the positions of three buoys: *A*, *B* and *C*.

(a) What is the bearing of *B* from *A*?

Answer .... *(1 mark)*

A racing yacht is anchored:

(i) along the bisector of angle *ABC*;

(ii) along the bisector of angle *ACB*.

(b) By drawing the loci of **(i)** and **(ii)** mark clearly the position of the yacht.

(4 marks)

Bearings & Loci

S48 The diagram shows the position of two electricity pylons, X and Y.
David is standing at Z.

Scale: 1 cm to 1 km

(a) What is the bearing of Y from X ?

Answer .... *(1 mark)*

(b) What is the actual distance of Y from Z ?

....

Answer .... km *(2 marks)*

David can see his friend Rupinder at A. Rupinder is further north than David.
Rupinder is equidistant from X and Y and is 5 km from David.

(c) Mark the position of A with a cross. *(3 marks)*

S49 Below is a scale drawing of an outdoor triangular-shaped swimming pool.
The scale is 1 cm to 5 m.

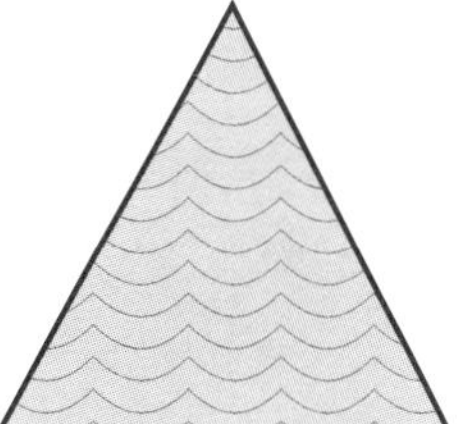

To stop grass growing within 12 m of the pool some organic weedkiller is to be sprayed next to the pool.

Shade on the diagram the area in which the weedkiller should be sprayed.

(3 marks)

S50

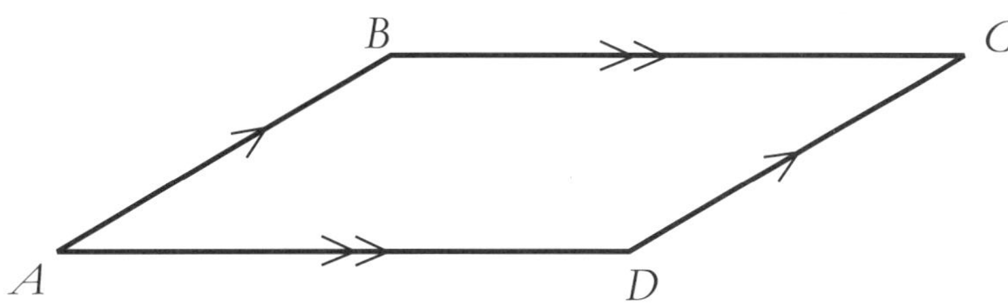

Draw accurately the locus of points that are 2 cm from the edge of the parallelogram *ABCD*.

(2 marks)

Rounding & Estimating

S51 A vet weighed a dog on scales that were accurate to the nearest 10 g. The display showed the dog's weight as 32.49 kg.

(a) What is the maximum that the dog could have weighed?

....

Answer .... kg *(1 mark)*

(b) What is the minimum that the dog could have weighed?

....

Answer .... kg *(1 mark)*

S52 A javelin was thrown 52.4 m to the nearest 10 cm.

(a) What is the maximum distance that the javelin could have been thrown?

....

Answer .... m *(1 mark)*

(b) What is the minimum distance that the javelin could have been thrown?

....

Answer .... m *(1 mark)*

S53 *ABCD* is a rectangle of length 7.2 cm and width 4.5 cm, both correct to 1 decimal place.

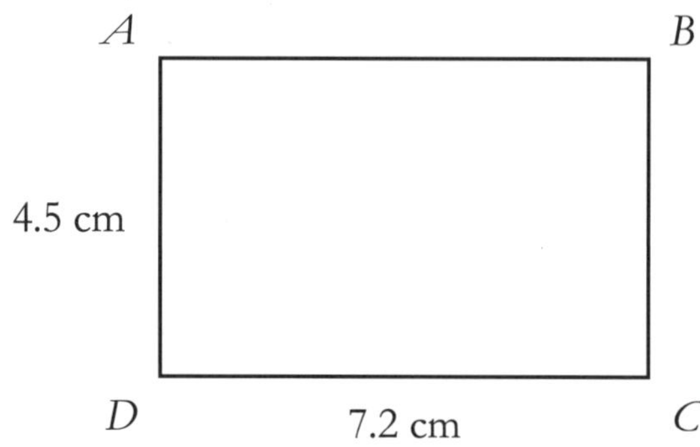

Not to scale

Calculate the upper bound and the lower bound for the area of the rectangle *ABCD*.

....

....

....

....

Upper bound = ...

Lower bound = ... *(5 marks)*

S54 **(a)** The radius of a cone is given by the formula $r = \frac{A}{\pi l}$.
If $A = 4.65$ cm^2 correct to 2 decimal places and $l = 2.5$ cm correct to 1 decimal place, work out the upper bound for the radius of the cone. Give your answer in terms of π.

....

....

....

Answer .... cm *(3 marks)*

(b) The formula for the volume of a cone is $V = \frac{1}{3}\pi r^2 h$.
If $r = 9.58$ cm and $h = 2.43$ cm, both correct to 2 decimal places, work out the lower bound for the volume of the cone. Give you answer in terms of π.

....

....

....

Answer .... cm^3 *(3 marks)*

Handling Data

Mean, Median, Mode, Range

H1 **(a)** Sakina measures the diameters of some beef tomatoes.
The diameters, in mm, are:

80, 82, 82, 83, 85, 89, 91, 92, 92, 94

(i) What is the range of the diameters of the beef tomatoes?

....

Answer .... mm *(1 mark)*

(ii) What is the mean diameter of the beef tomatoes?

....

....

Answer .... mm *(3 marks)*

To compare, Sakina measures the diameters of some plum tomatoes.
The range of these diameters is 18 mm and the mean 62 mm.

(b) Comment on the differences between these two varieties.

....

....*(1 mark)*

H2 **(a)** Donald weighs some English Red apples.
The weights, in grams, are listed below.

55, 56, 56, 57, 59, 60, 62, 63, 63, 64, 65

(i) What is the range of weights for the English Red apples?

....

Answer .... g *(1 mark)*

(ii) What is the mean weight of the English Red apples?

....

....

Answer .... g *(3 marks)*

Donald then weighs some South African Green apples. The range of these weights is 16 g and the mean is 60 g.

(b) Comment on similarities and differences between these two varieties of apples.

....

....*(1 mark)*

H3 The weights of 9 badminton players are shown below.

75 kg, 81 kg, 74 kg, 84 kg, 74 kg, 78 kg, 83 kg, 74 kg, 83 kg

(a) Find their median weight.

....

Answer .... kg *(2 marks)*

(b) Find the mode of their weights.

Answer .... kg *(1 mark)*

(c) Which of the above is not a good indicator of their average weight? Why?

....*(1 mark)*

H4 Luke carried out a survey of how much money 8 of his friends had deposited in their savings accounts. The amounts were £47, £55, £63, £57, £82, £4002, £55 and £12.

(a) What was the mean amount deposited?

....

Answer £.. *(3 marks)*

(b) Find the median.

....

Answer £.. *(2 marks)*

(c) Look at your answers to **(a)** and **(b)**. Which does not give a good indication of the average savings of the 8 friends? Explain your answer.

....

....*(1 mark)*

H5 The table shows the number of employees working for a walking boot manufacturer over a three-year period.

	March	June	September	December
1955	68	78	72	42
1956	62	72	75	38
1957	57	64	68	36

(a) Plot the data as a time series on the graph paper below.

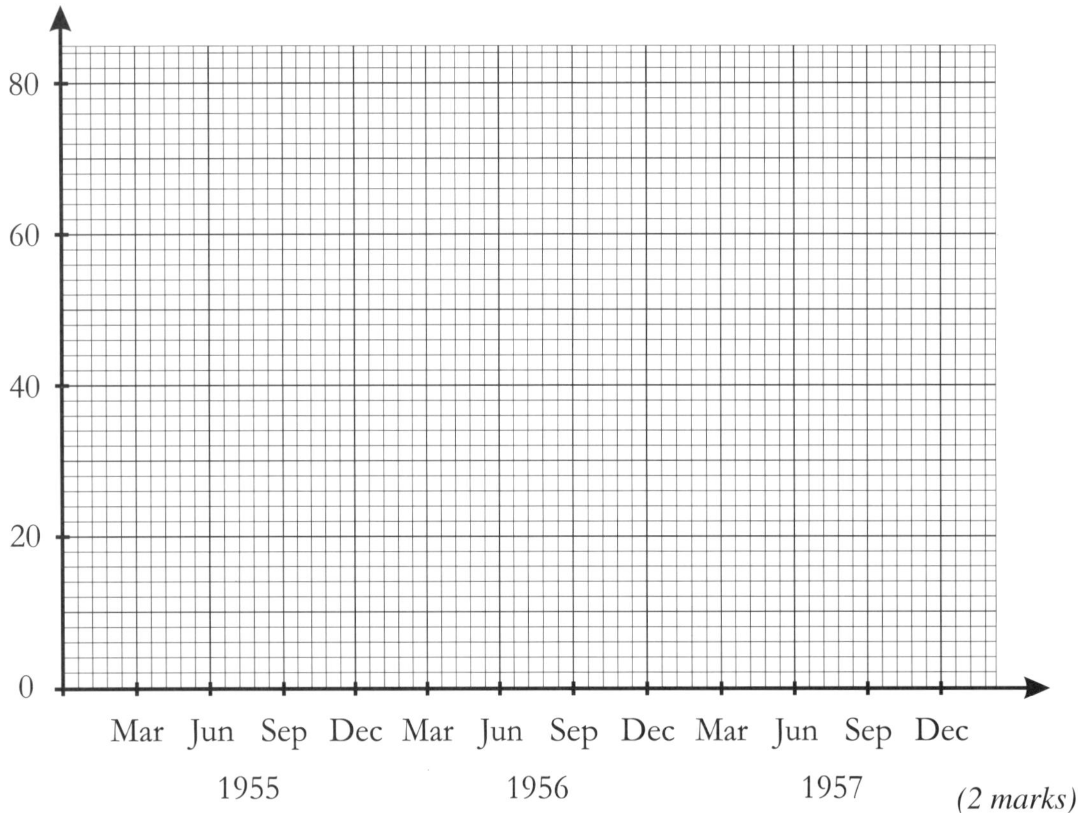

(2 marks)

(b) Calculate the four-point moving average and plot it on the same graph.

....

.... *(3 marks)*

(c) Comment on your graph.

....

.... *(2 marks)*

H6 The frequency table below shows the number of goals scored by 40 non-league football teams one Saturday afternoon.

Number of Teams	11	13	9	5	2
Number of Goals	0	1	2	3	4

(a) Calculate the mean number of goals per team.

....

....

Answer .... *(2 marks)*

(b) What is the modal number of goals scored per team?

Answer .... *(1 mark)*

H7 The table below shows the number of eggs laid by 100 different hens.

Number of Hens	Number of Eggs
18	0
32	1
26	2
12	3
8	4
4	5

(a) Calculate the mean number of eggs laid per hen.

....

....

Answer .... *(2 marks)*

(b) What is the modal number of eggs laid?

Answer .... *(1 mark)*

(c) What is the median number of eggs laid?

....

Answer .... *(1 mark)*

H8 The deputy manager of a garden centre measured the heights of 24 rose bushes. Below is his data in cm.

52	54	59	43	50	51	52	53	49	47	46	53
49	42	58	56	44	52	48	51	49	47	46	53

(a) Complete the grouped frequency table for the heights of the rose bushes.

Height (h cm)	Tally	Frequency
$40 \leqslant h < 44$		
$44 \leqslant h < 48$		
$48 \leqslant h < 52$		
$52 \leqslant h < 56$		
$56 \leqslant h < 60$		

(2 marks)

(b) Draw a frequency polygon to represent the data.

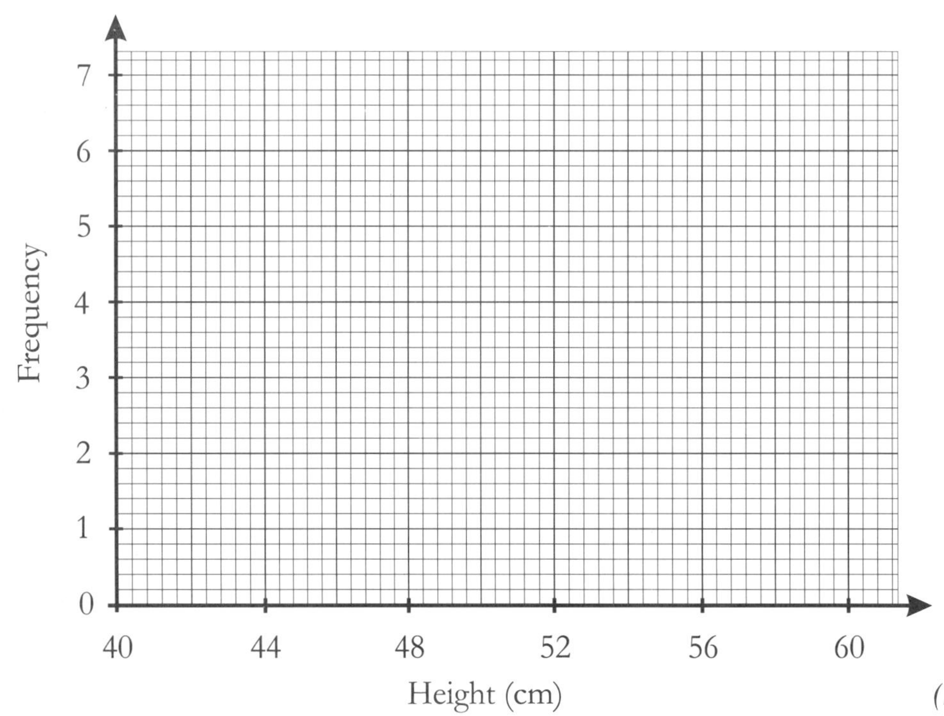

(2 marks)

H9 Geoff timed how long his racing pigeons took to return home after being released some distance away. His data, in minutes, is recorded below.

43	30	50	55	46	37	52	47	41	49
53	44	49	43	50	41	59	45	48	47
47	40	45	58	33	34	42	49	36	43

(a) Complete the grouped frequency table for the times.

Time (T mins)	Tally	Frequency
$30 \leqslant T < 36$		
$36 \leqslant T < 42$		
$42 \leqslant T < 48$		
$48 \leqslant T < 54$		
$54 \leqslant T < 60$		

(2 marks)

(b) Draw the frequency polygon for the times on the graph paper below.

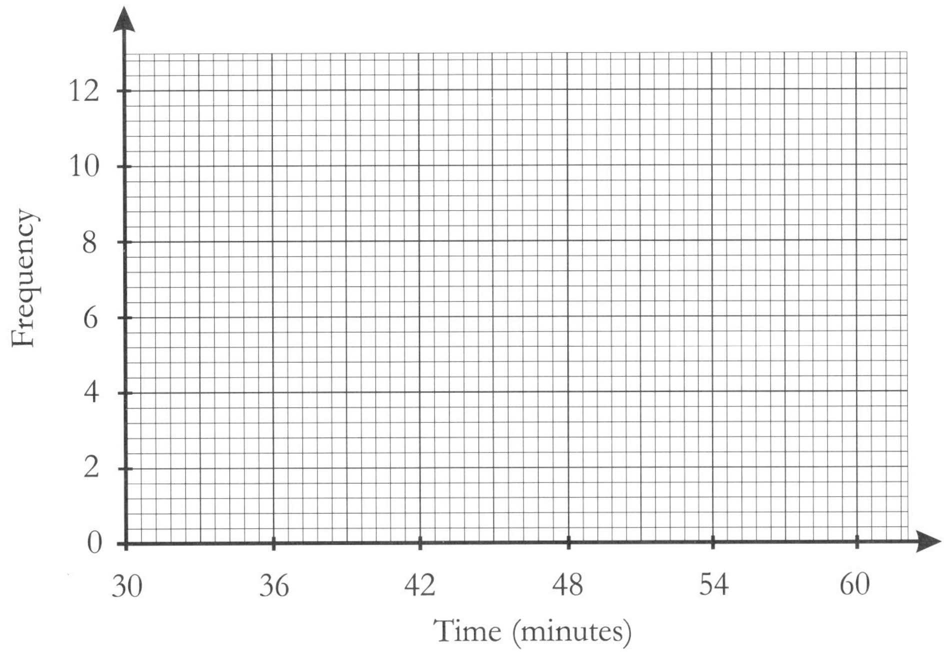

(2 marks)

Cumulative Frequency

H10 This cumulative frequency curve shows the lengths of time that some people spent in a supermarket.

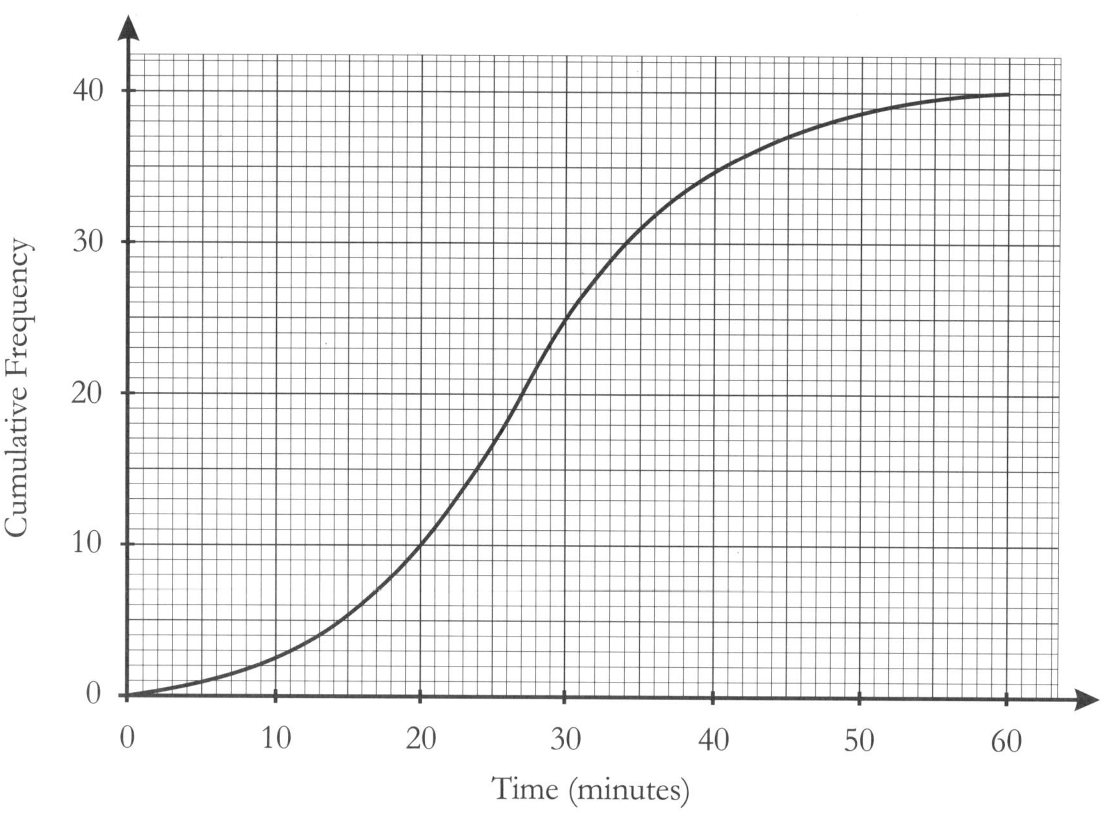

(a) How many people took part in the survey?

Answer .... people *(1 mark)*

(b) Find the median time spent in the supermarket.

Answer .... mins *(2 marks)*

(c) How many people spent longer than 20 minutes in the supermarket?

....

Answer .... people *(2 marks)*

(d) Find the interquartile range.

....

....

Answer .... mins *(3 marks)*

H11 The graph shows the amount of money spent on eating out, by a group of families each month.

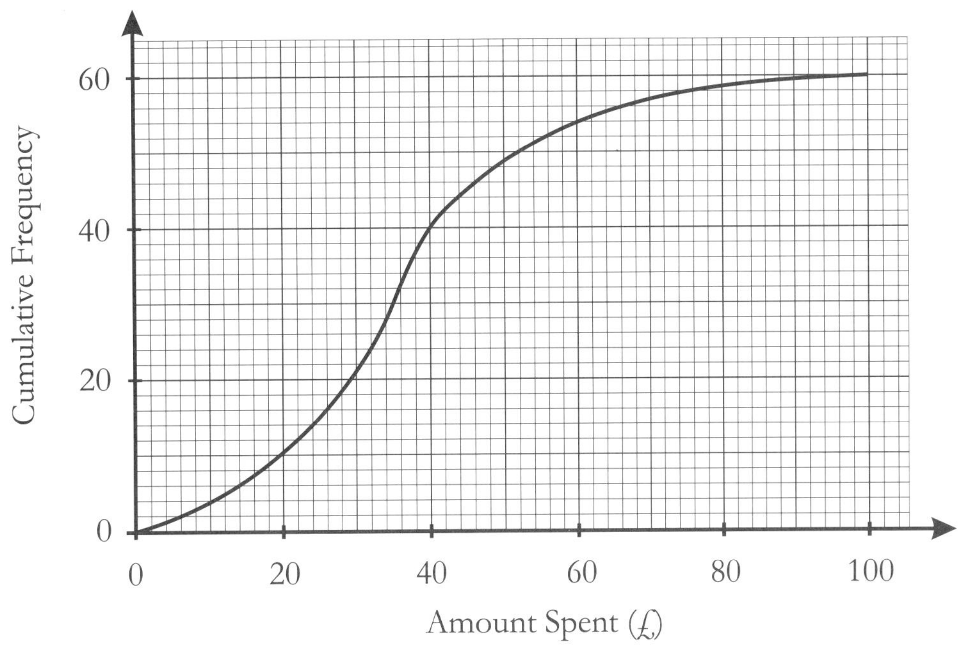

(a) How many families were surveyed?

Answer .... families *(1 mark)*

(b) Find the median amount spent.

Answer £ .... *(2 marks)*

(c) What percentage of families spent less than £40 per month on eating out?

....

Answer .... % *(2 marks)*

(d) Work out the interquartile range of the data.

....

....

Answer £ .... *(3 marks)*

Cumulative Frequency

H12 Colin is looking for a new front door for his house. He has compiled a table of the prices of 240 front doors as shown.

Price (£P)	**Number**
$500 \leqslant P < 550$	4
$550 \leqslant P < 600$	30
$600 \leqslant P < 650$	50
$650 \leqslant P < 700$	96
$700 \leqslant P < 750$	50
$750 \leqslant P < 800$	10

(a) Use Colin's data to complete the cumulative frequency table below.

£P less than	**Number**
500	0
550	4
600	
650	
700	
750	
800	

(1 mark)

(b) Use the graph paper provided to draw a cumulative frequency graph of the data.

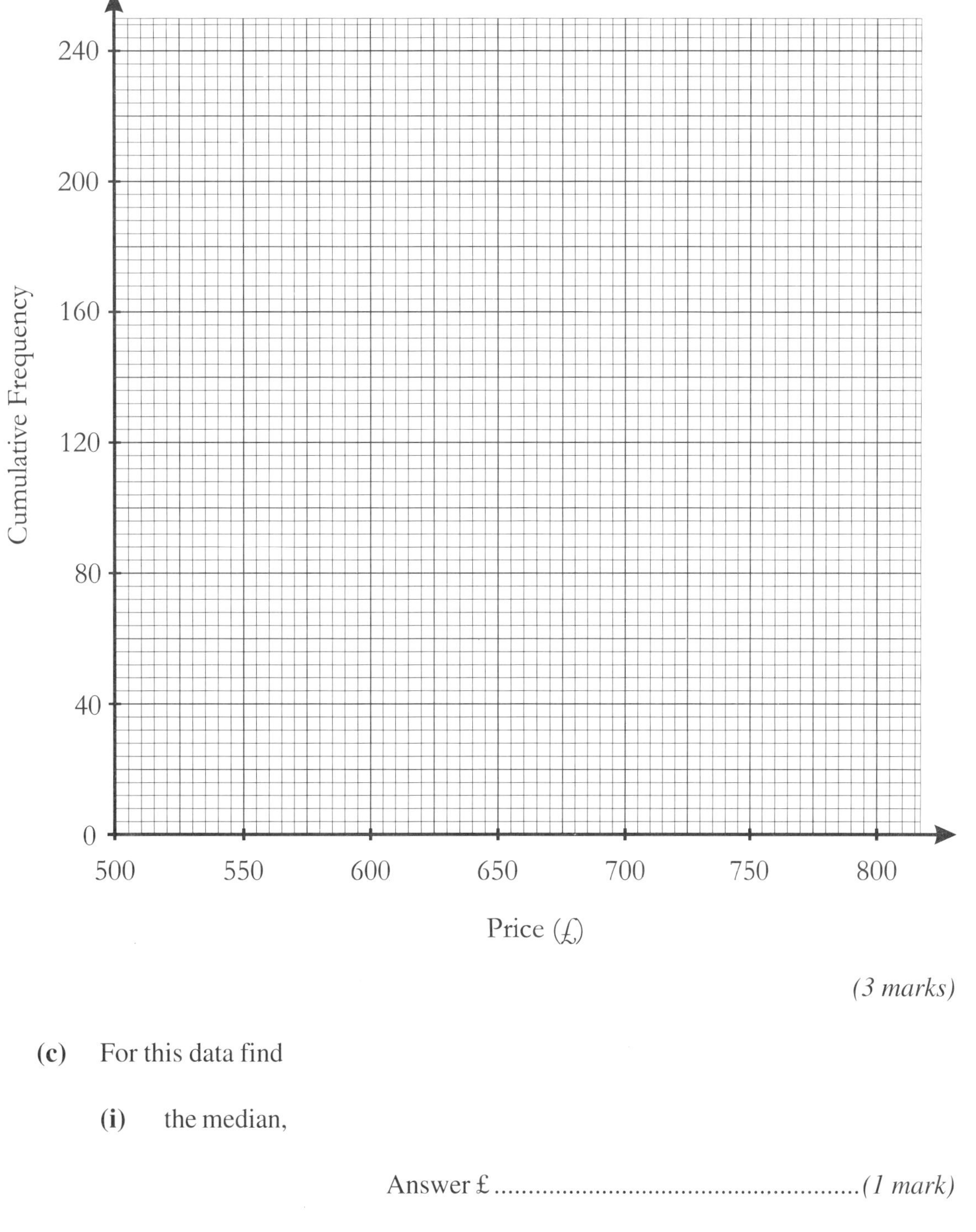

(3 marks)

(c) For this data find

(i) the median,

Answer £ .... *(1 mark)*

(ii) the interquartile range.

....

Answer £ .... *(2 marks)*

Cumulative Frequency

H13 The times taken by 160 people to complete an IQ test are shown, in minutes, in the table below.

Time (t mins)	Number
$40 \leqslant t < 50$	8
$50 \leqslant t < 60$	28
$60 \leqslant t < 70$	64
$70 \leqslant t < 80$	40
$80 \leqslant t < 90$	15
$90 \leqslant t < 100$	5

(a) Fill in the cumulative frequency table.

Time (t mins)	Cumulative Frequency
$t < 40$	0
$t < 50$	
$t < 60$	
$t < 70$	
$t < 80$	
$t < 90$	
$t < 100$	

(1 mark)

(b) Draw a cumulative frequency curve for the data, using the graph paper provided.

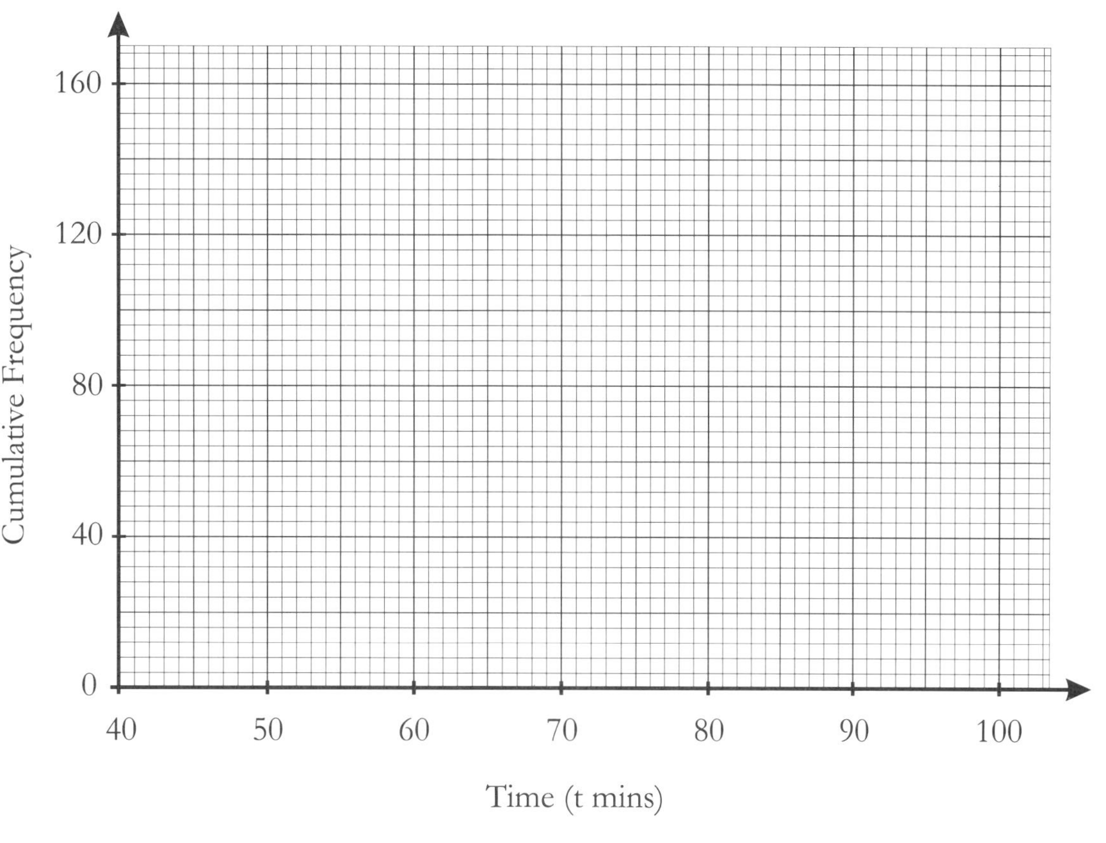

(3 marks)

(c) Estimate the median.

Answer .... mins *(1 mark)*

(d) Use your graph to estimate the number of people who took longer than 65 minutes.

....

Answer .... people *(2 marks)*

(e) Find the interquartile range.

....

Answer .... mins *(2 marks)*

Box Plots

H14 Inder drew this box-and-whisker diagram to show the length of time that people spent waiting to log onto the Internet.

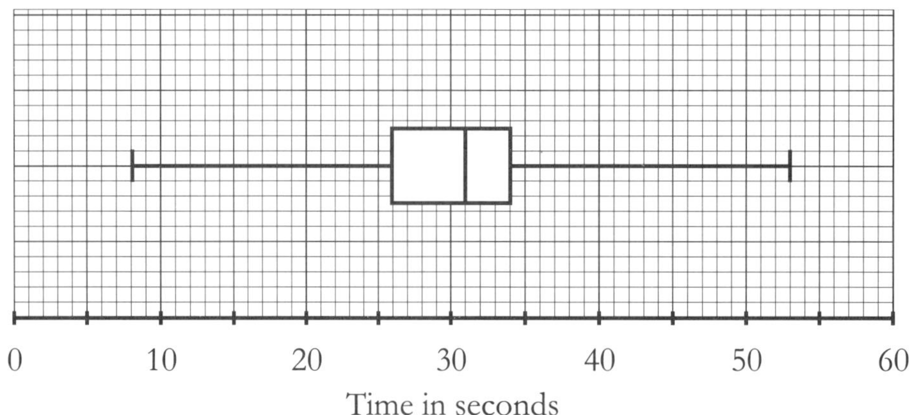

Copy and complete this table.

	Minimum	Maximum	Median	Lower quartile	Upper quartile
Time in seconds					

(2 marks)

H15 The speeds in miles per hour of 14 tennis serves were recorded.
The speeds were:

102, 87, 90, 68, 95, 121, 56, 78, 83, 109, 86, 76, 63, 81.

(a) Draw a box-and-whisker diagram to show the data.

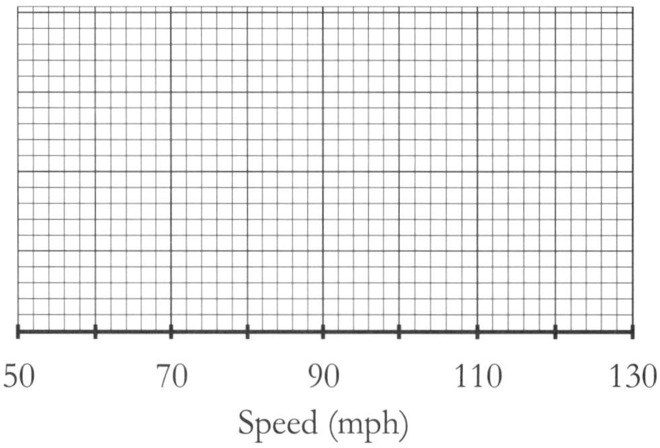

(b) Describe the skewness of the distribution.

....

....*(1 mark)*

H16 The table shows the price of 9 cars, together with their top speeds in mph.

Price (£1000s)	12	26	32	15	18	8	22	41	43
Top Speed (mph)	90	114	124	93	101	85	111	131	139

(a) Draw a scatter graph to show this information.

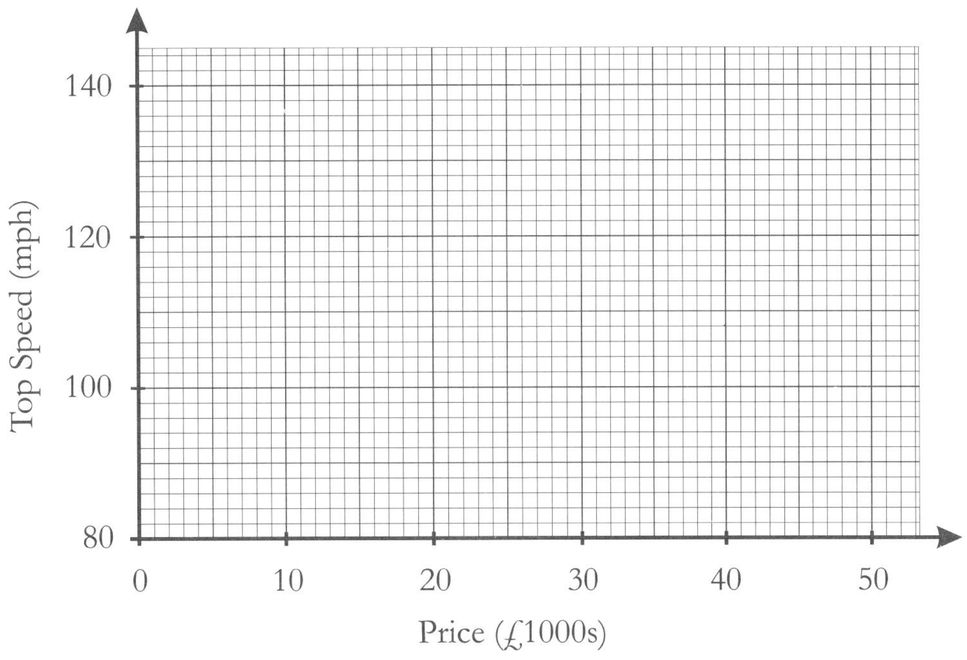

(2 marks)

(b) Describe the correlation between the price of these cars and their top speeds.

....*(1 mark)*

(c) Draw a line of best fit on your scatter graph. *(1 mark)*

(d) Use your line of best fit to estimate

(i) the price of a car with a top speed of 120 mph,

Answer £...*(1 mark)*

(ii) the top speed of a car costing £25 000.

Answer .... mph *(1 mark)*

Scatter Graphs

H17

Height (cm)	10	37	31	12	23	22	14	27	16	20
Amount (ml)	23	8	10	22	14	15	21	12	19	16

The table above shows the heights of some fully grown tomato plants and the amount of Thunder Growth Feed given to them each day.

(a) Draw a scatter graph to show this information.

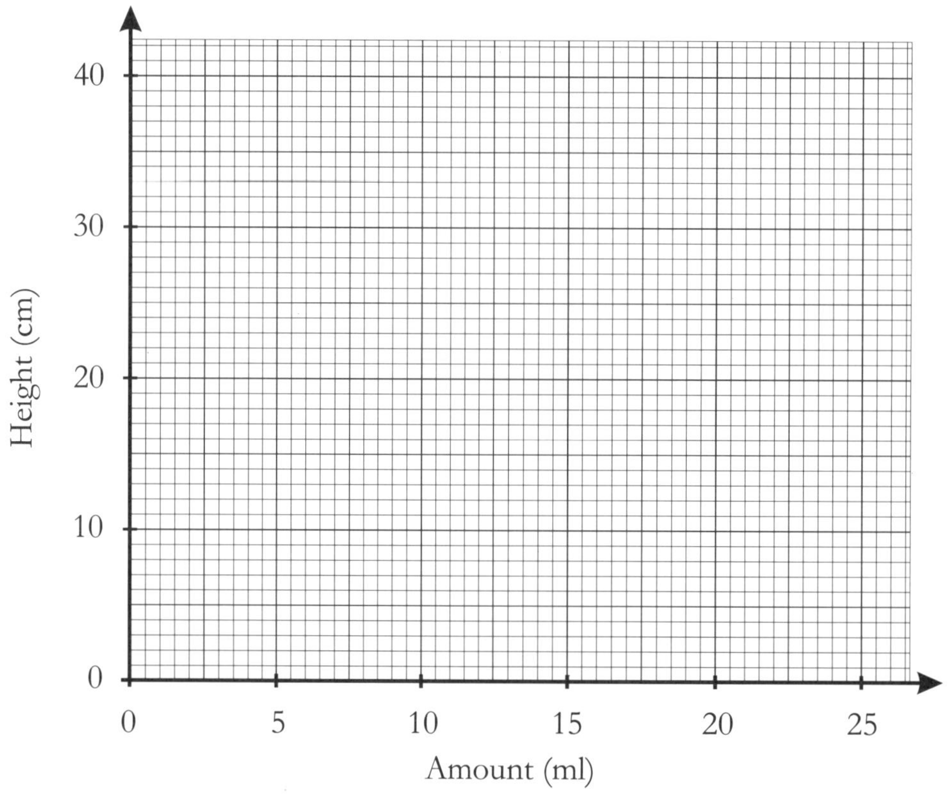

(2 marks)

(b) Draw a line of best fit on your scatter graph. *(1 mark)*

(c) Use your line to estimate the height of a fully grown tomato plant fed 5 ml of Thunder Growth Feed each day.

Answer .... cm *(1 mark)*

(d) Describe the correlation between the amount of Thunder Growth Feed given and the height.

.... *(1 mark)*

H18 The table and histogram show how long (in minutes) 100 people spent watching television one evening.

Time (t mins)	Frequency
$0 \leqslant t < 15$	10
$15 \leqslant t < 30$	
$30 \leqslant t < 60$	40
$60 \leqslant t < 120$	
$120 \leqslant t < 180$	10
$t > 180$	0

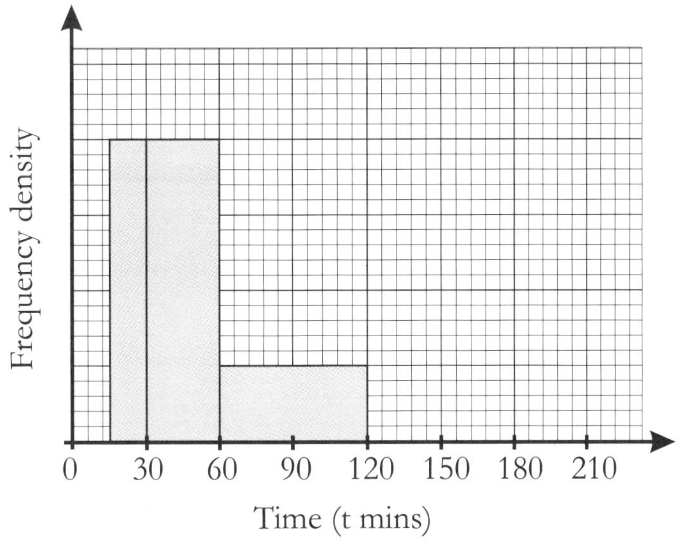

(a) Use the information in the histogram to complete the table. *(3 marks)*

(b) Use the information in the table to complete the histogram. *(2 marks)*

Histograms

H19 The table shows the length of time that people waited to use a cash machine one morning.

Time in seconds	Frequency
$0 \leqslant x < 5$	10
$5 \leqslant x < 15$	16
$15 \leqslant x < 25$	18
$25 \leqslant x < 30$	20
$30 \leqslant x < 50$	36
$50 \leqslant x < 60$	12

(a) On the grid, draw a histogram to represent this information.

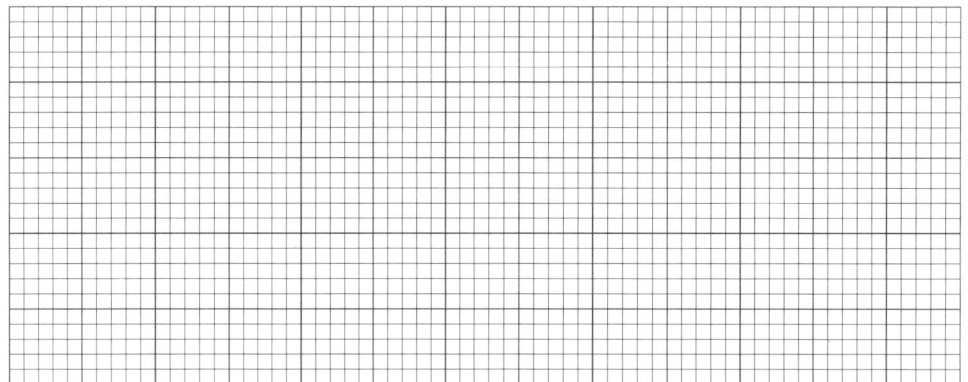

(3 marks)

(b) Calculate an estimate of the mean waiting time.

....

....

....

....

Answer .... *(2 marks)*

H20 A biased spinner has 3 sides labelled *A*, *B* and *C*. During 2 experiments, the spinner is spun and the results recorded.

Experiment	Total No. of Spins	*A*	*B*	*C*
1	100	38	7	55
2	1000	402	99	499

(a) Use the results from the first experiment to estimate the probability of the spinner landing on *A*.

....

Answer .... *(1 mark)*

(b) Use the results from the second experiment to estimate the probability of the spinner landing on *A*.

....

Answer .... *(1 mark)*

The spinner is spun 5000 times in a third experiment.

(c) Estimate the number of times the spinner will land on *A*. Use your answers to **(a)** and **(b)** to justify your answer.

....

.... *(2 marks)*

H21 A biased dice, with faces numbered 1, 2, 3, 4, 5 and 6, is thrown 500 times. The results are shown in the table below.

Number	1	2	3	4	5	6
Frequency	45	248	2	55	94	56

(a) Estimate the probability that the next time the dice is thrown it will show a 2.

....

Answer .... *(1 mark)*

Estimate the probability that the next time the dice is thrown it will show:

(b) an odd number

....

Answer .... *(2 marks)*

(c) a number greater than 4.

....

Answer .... *(2 marks)*

H22 Steven always has one piece of fruit with his lunch. The table below shows the probability that he has a particular fruit with his lunch.

Applc	Pear	Banana	Peach	Grapes
0.3	0.2	0.1	0.3	0.1

(a) Calculate the probability of Steven not having an apple with his lunch.

....

Answer ....*(1 mark)*

(b) Calculate the probability of Steven having an apple or a pear.

....

Answer .... *(2 marks)*

H23 Sandra has estimated the probabilities of it raining on particular days of the year. Her estimates are shown in the table below.

St Valentine's Day	Easter Sunday	May Day	Christmas Day
0.5	0.3	0.2	0.7

(a) Use the table to calculate the probability of it not raining on May Day.

....

Answer ....*(1 mark)*

(b) Calculate the probability of it raining on Easter Sunday and Christmas Day.

....

Answer .... *(2 marks)*

(c) Calculate the probability of it not raining on Valentine's Day or Christmas Day.

....

Answer .... *(2 marks)*

H24 Sonia has a cold. The probability that her sister Amy will catch a cold is 0.42. The probability that her brother Jack will catch a cold is 0.16.

(a) What is the probability that both Amy and Jack will catch colds?

....

Answer .... *(2 marks)*

(b) What is the probability that neither of them will catch colds?

....

....

Answer .... *(3 marks)*

(c) What is the probability that at least one of them will catch a cold?

....

Answer .... *(2 marks)*

H25 Roberta has 2 biased dice. The probability that dice *A* will land on a six is 0.25. The probability that dice *B* will land on a six is 0.12. Roberta throws both dice just once.

(a) What is the probability of Roberta throwing 2 sixes?

....

Answer .... *(2 marks)*

(b) What is the probability that Roberta will throw no more than 1 six?

....

Answer .... *(2 marks)*

H26 A bag contains 6 green balls, 4 red balls and 2 blue balls.

(a) If 2 balls are picked at random, what is the probability that they are both blue?

....

Answer .... *(2 marks)*

(b) If 3 balls are picked at random, what is the probability that 2 of them are blue?

....

....

....

Answer .... *(3 marks)*

(c) 4 balls are picked at random. From these, 2 balls are randomly selected. What is the probability that these 2 balls are both blue?

....

....

....

Answer .... *(4 marks)*

H27 Six cards from an ordinary pack of playing cards have been placed face down on a table. Three of the cards are aces, two are red queens and one is the king of spades.

(a) If a card is picked out at random, what is the probability that it is the queen of hearts?

....

Answer .... *(1 mark)*

(b) If three cards are picked at random, what is the probability that two of them are red queens?

....

....

Answer .... *(3 marks)*

Gareth randomly selects a card and removes it from the table.

(c) If Pam now selects three cards, what is the probability that they are all aces?

....

Answer .... *(3 marks)*

H28 Robina, Suzy, Roger and Harry are playing a board game. The probabilities of Robina, Suzy, Roger or Harry being first to complete a circuit of the board are as follows:

Robina	Suzy	Roger	Harry
0.25	0.32	0.17	0.26

After the first circuit, the player who completed the circuit first has a probability of 0.45 of winning.

(a) Use the information above to complete the tree diagram.

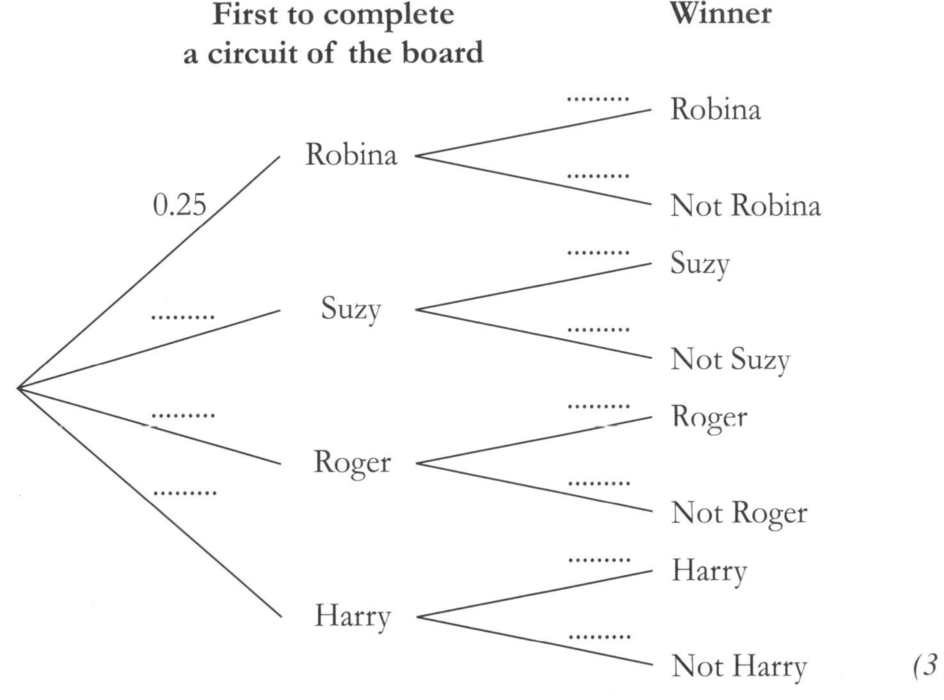

(3 marks)

(b) Calculate the probability that Suzy will be the first to complete a circuit, yet lose the game.

....

....

Answer .... *(2 marks)*

H29 Charlotte and Brian usually go shopping together on Friday evenings. The probability that Charlotte goes shopping on any particular Friday evening is 0.96. If Charlotte goes shopping, the probability that Brian will go as well is 0.82. If Charlotte doesn't go, the probability that Brian will still go is 0.68.

(a) Use the above information to complete the tree diagram.

Charlotte **Brian**

....

....

....

....

....

....

(3 marks)

(b) What is the probability that Brian will go shopping alone?

....

....

Answer .... *(2 marks)*

(c) What is the probability that at least one of them will go shopping?

....

....

....

Answer .... *(3 marks)*

H30 A council is conducting a survey to see what traffic calming measures are required in a particular area. To do this, they plan to take a 10% sample of households from the streets concerned.

(a) Give one advantage of using a sample.

....*(1 mark)*

(b) Give one disadvantage of using a sample.

....*(1 mark)*

(c) Suggest a suitable sampling method which the council might use.

....*(1 mark)*

(d) Explain the advantages of the type of sample you have suggested in part **(c)**.

....

.... *(2 marks)*

H31 A health authority is conducting a survey to find out how often people visit the dentist. To do this they decide to take a sample of 1000 people.

(a) Describe how the health authority might select a random sample.

....

.... *(2 marks)*

(b) Suggest another sampling method which might more accurately reflect the population.

....*(1 mark)*

(c) Explain how the health authority could use the sampling method you suggested in **(b)**.

....

.... *(2 marks)*

Answers

NUMBER

N1 (a) £301.32 (b) 27

N2 (a) £527.62 (b) 31

N3 (a) 258 m (b) 86 m

N4 (a) 24°C
(b) Sweden -20°C
France -5°C

N5 $\frac{24}{360} = \frac{1}{15}$

N6 $\frac{5}{30} = \frac{1}{6}$

N7 (a) $\frac{15}{100} = \frac{3}{20}$ (b) 15
(c) 0.0015 (d) 32

N8 (a) 2, 4, 6, 10 (b) 2, 10
(c) $x = 10$, $y = 6$

N9 (a) 84 (b) 4

N10 (a) 850 (b) 12

N11 28 m

N12 24 cm

N13 (a) 87.5% (b) 12.5%

N14 (a) 62.5% (b) 37.5%

N15 £15

N16 (a) £35 (b) 36.4%

N17 (a) £23 (b) £28.75

N18 £2.28

N19 (a) 120 g (b) 37.5%

N20 (a) 480 g (b) 75%

N21 (a) £10 200 (b) £8670

N22 (a) £42.40 (b) £44.94

N23 12.9%

N24 23.8%

N25 (a) £62 609 (b) £71 579

N26 (a) £1091 (b) £1143

N27 32.25%

N28 32%

N29 (a) 4.83 (b) 1.58 (c) 0.422

N30 (a) $\frac{1}{2}$ (b) 8 (c) 25

N31 $y = 0$

N32 $x = 2$

N33 (a) 27 (b) 9, 16
(c) 10 (d) $x = 9$, $y = 27$

N34 $x = 3$, $y = 13$, $z = 16$

N35 (a) 252 (b) $2 \times 3^2 \times 5$

N36 (a) $5^2 \times 11$ (b) $x = 2, y = 2, z = 1$

N37 (a) $2\pi, \sqrt{12}$ (b) e.g. 14.44 ($= 3.8^2$)
(c) e.g. $\sqrt{3}$ and $\frac{1}{\sqrt{3}}$

N38 (a) $\frac{3}{5}$, 11.2 (b) e.g. 10.648 ($= 2.2^3$)
(c) e.g. $12\sqrt{2}$ and $\frac{1}{\sqrt{2}}$

N39 $\frac{31}{99}$

N40 $\frac{142}{333}$

N41 (a) $3\sqrt{2}$ (b) $5 + 2\sqrt{3}$

N42 (a) 1.14 (b) 1.1

N43 (a) 1.222 (b) 1.22

N44 (a) $\frac{20 \times 50}{500} = 2$
(b) Surface area $\approx 4 \times 3 \times 5^2 = 300$ m^2
There won't be enough paint.

N45 (a) $\frac{400 \times 0.5}{40} = 5$
(b) Surface area $\approx 6 \times 30^2 = 5400$ cm^2
There won't be enough paint.

N46 0.022 to 2 s.f.

N47 0.02 to 1 s.f.

N48 25 000 m

N49 110 pounds

N50 (a) \$420
(b) £28.57 (to the nearest penny)

N51 (a) Drc243 600
(b) £4.43 (to the nearest penny)

A1 (a) 9.2×10^5 (b) 4 300 000

A2 (a) 4.42×10^5 (b) 6.37×10^6

A3 (a) 8.5×10^8
(b) $(3 \times 10^6) \div (8.5 \times 10^8) = 3.5 \times 10^{-3}$ (to 2 s.f.)

A4 (a) 3.84×10^5
(b) 110 Moon diameters

A5 (a) $6.2 \times 10^2 \times 7.4 \times 10^{-3} = 4.6$ cm (to 2 s.f.)
(b) $(4.2 \times 10^2) \div (6.2 \times 10^2)$
$= 0.68$ g or 6.8×10^{-1} g (to 2 s.f.)

A6 (a) 13 (b) 3.3

A7 (a) $x = 1\frac{1}{5}$ (b) $x = 4$ (c) $x = 1$
(d) $x = 15$ (e) $x = 12$

A8 (a) $y = 4\frac{1}{11}$ (b) $y = 2$ (c) $y = 3$
(d) $y = 2$ (e) $y = 12$

A9 (a) $4x + 8 = 32$ (b) £6

A10 (a) $4y + 12 = 852$ (b) 210 g

A11 (a) 15 (b) 32

A12 (a) $\frac{2}{9}$ (b) 11

A13 (a) $T = 20W + 20$ (b) 3 hours

A14 (a) $P = £(6H + 2S)$ (b) £72

A15 $a = \sqrt{(b - 2)}$

A16 $x = \frac{y^{1/3} - 4}{3}$

A17 (a) $b = \frac{a}{2c^2}$ (b) $c = \sqrt{\frac{a}{2b}}$

A18 (a) $a = \frac{v^2 - u^2}{2s}$ (b) $u = \sqrt{(v^2 - 2as)}$

A19 **(a)** $3x^4$ **(b)** $\dfrac{x^2 + 2x}{6}$ **(c)** $x = 1$

A20 **(a)** $\dfrac{x^2}{2}$ **(b)** $2x^2$ **(c)** $x = 6$

A21 **(a)** $a = \dfrac{c}{bc - 1}$ **(b)** $\dfrac{13x + 6}{(x + 2)(x - 3)}$

A22 **(a)** $x = \dfrac{1 + y}{yz}$ **(b)** $\dfrac{16x + 6}{(x + 1)(2x + 1)}$

A23 **(a)** $y = 2.5$ **(b)** -0.5

(c)

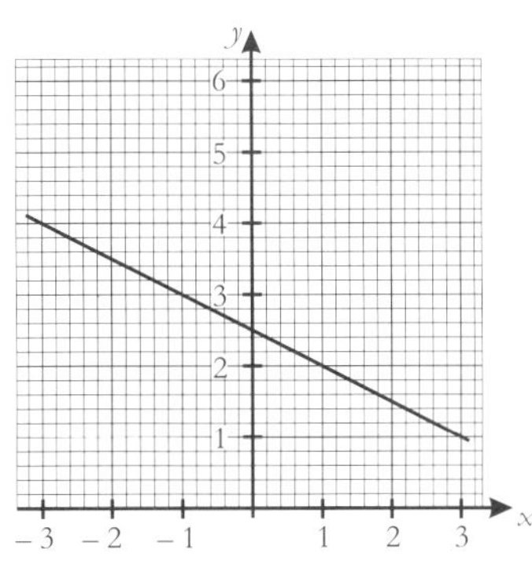

A24 **(a)**

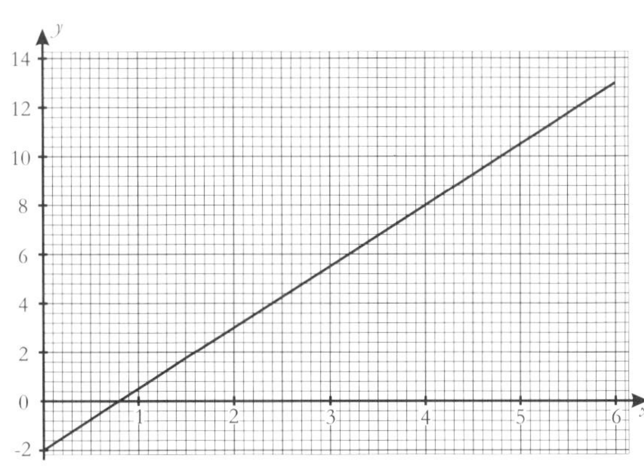

(b) $y = 8$ **(c)** $x = 5.2$

A25

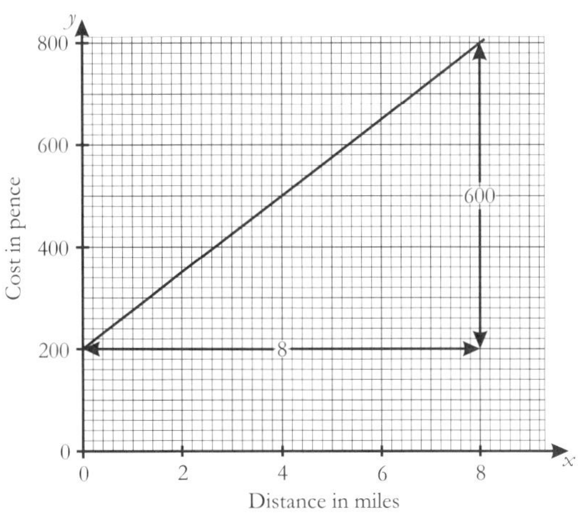

(a) Gradient = $\dfrac{600}{8}$ = 75,

y-intercept = 200,

so $y = 75x + 200$.

(b) $75 \times 10 + 200 = 950\text{p} = £9.50$

A26 **(a)** $6y = 3x + 8$ **(b)** $2y + 4x = 3$

A27 $y = 3x - 3$

A28 $y = 17 - 4x$

A29 **(a)**

Time (T, minutes)	1	2	3	4	5
Mass (M, grams)	9.2	7.8	6.6	5.7	4.9
0.8^T	0.8	0.64	0.51	0.41	0.33

(b)

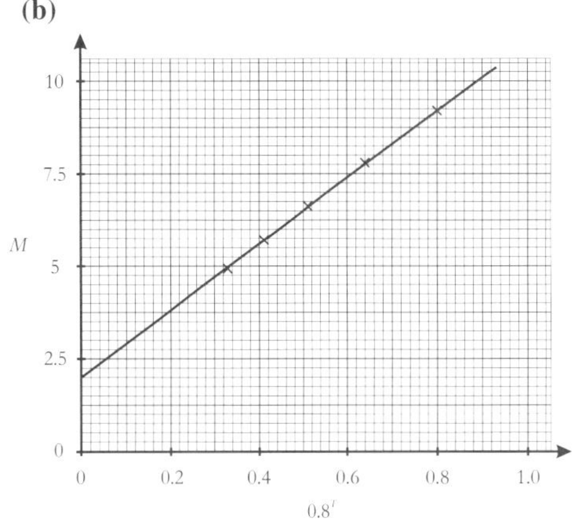

(c) a = gradient = 9, b = y-intercept = 2

(d) $9 \times (0.8)^0 + 2 = 11$ g

A30 $x = -4.5$, $y = 4$

A31 $x = -2$, $y = 3$

A32 **(a)** $x = 2$, $y = 1$

(b)

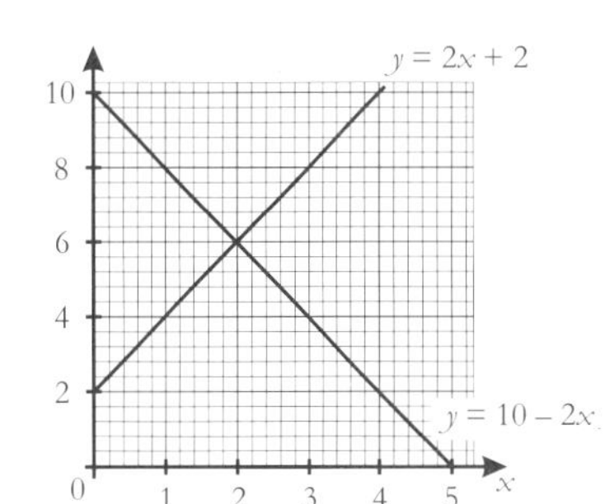

(iii) The graphs meet where $x = 2$.

A33 **(a)** $x = 3$, $y = 1$

(b)

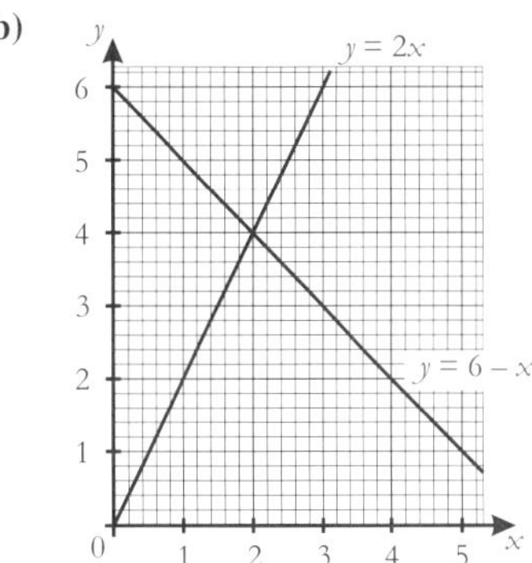

(iii) The graphs meet where $y = 4$.

A34 **(a)** $x^2 + y^2 = 16$ **(b)** (0, 4), (4, 0)

A35 (0, 5), (3, 4)

A36 (2, -5), (3, -3)

A37 -5, -4, -3, -2, -1, 0, 1, 2, 3

A38 -1, 0, 1, 2, 3, 4, 5, 6

A39 **(a)** $x < \frac{1}{2}$

(b) 

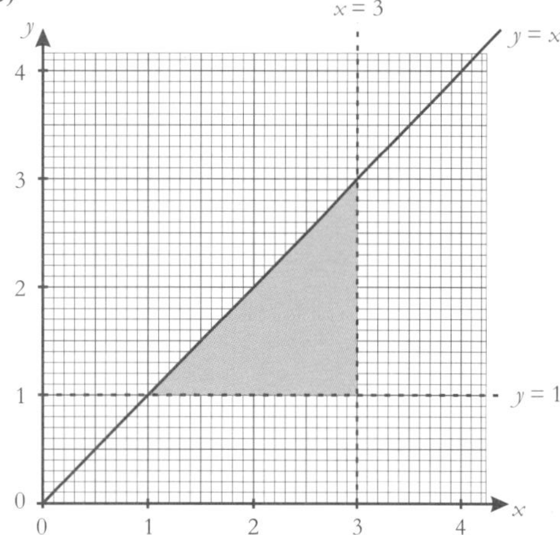

A40 **(a)** $x < 3\frac{1}{13}$

(b) 

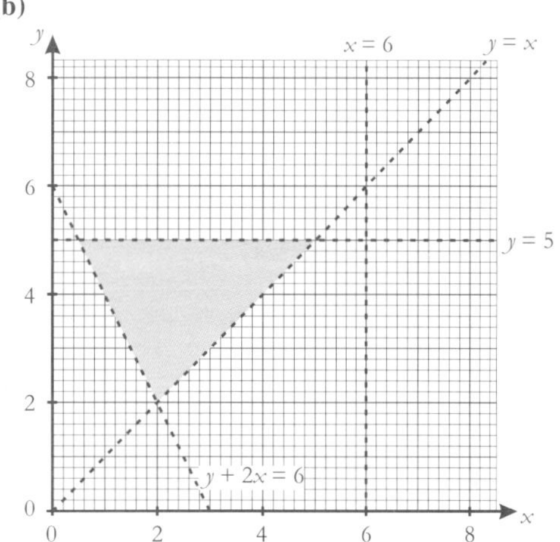

(c) (2, 3), (2, 4), (3, 4)

A41 **(a)** $x = 2.6$ **(b)** $x = 1.3$

A42 **(a)** $x = 4.4$ **(b)** $x = 1.9$

A43 **(a)** $2x^2 - 5x - 63$

(b) $3x^3 + 3x^2 + 6x$

(c) $(x + 2)(x + 3)$

A44 **(a)** $15x^2 + 2x - 8$

(b) $2x^3 + 3x^2 + 3x$

(c) $(x + 4)(x - 2)$

A45 $(3x + 4y)(3x - 4y)$

A46 $(x + 3y)(x - 3y)$

A47 $(x + 3)^2 + 3$

A48 $x^2 - 14x + 10 = (x - 7)^2 - 39$, so $a = 7$, $b = 39$

A49 $x = 0$ or $x = 4$

A50 $x = 0$ or $x = -3$

A51 $x^2 - x - 12 = (x - 4)(x + 3) = 0$, so $x = 4$ or -3

A52 $x^2 - 3x - 10 = (x - 5)(x + 2) = 0$, so $x = 5$ or -2

A53 **(a)** area $MNOP$ = area $ABCD$

$x \times (x + 2) = 1 \times (x + 6)$

$x^2 + 2x = x + 6$

$x^2 + x - 6 = 0$

(b) MP = 2 cm (-3 cm is a nonsensical solution)

A54 **(a)** $16 - x$ cm

(b) length × width = area

$x(16 - x) = 48$

$16x - x^2 = 48$

$x^2 - 16x + 48 = 0$

(c) Possible lengths are 4 cm and 12 cm.

A55 **(a)** $(x - 2)^2 + (x - 1)^2 = x^2$

giving $x^2 - 6x + 5 = 0$

(b) 5 cm ($x = 1$ gives a nonsensical solution)

A56 **(a)** $(x - 8)^2 + (x - 1)^2 = x^2$

giving $x^2 - 18x + 65 = 0$

(b) 13 cm ($x = 5$ gives a nonsensical solution)

A57 $x = 1.43$ or 0.23

A58 $x = -2.45$ or 0.204

A59 **(a)**

x	-2	-1	0	1	2	3
y	21	5	-3	-3	5	21

(b) 

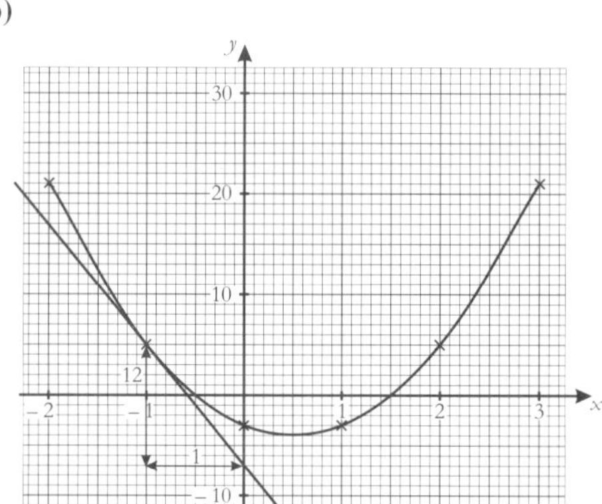

(c) $x = -0.5$ or $x = 1.5$

(d) Gradient of the curve at $x = -1$ is -12.

A60 **(a)**

x	-3	-2	-1	0	1	2	3
y	14	7	2	-1	-2	-1	2

(b)

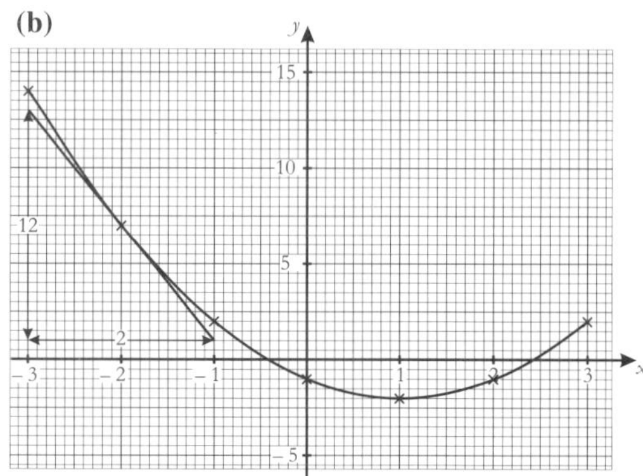

(c) $x = -0.4$ or $x = 2.4$

(d) Gradient of the curve at $x = -2$ is -6.

A61 **(a)**

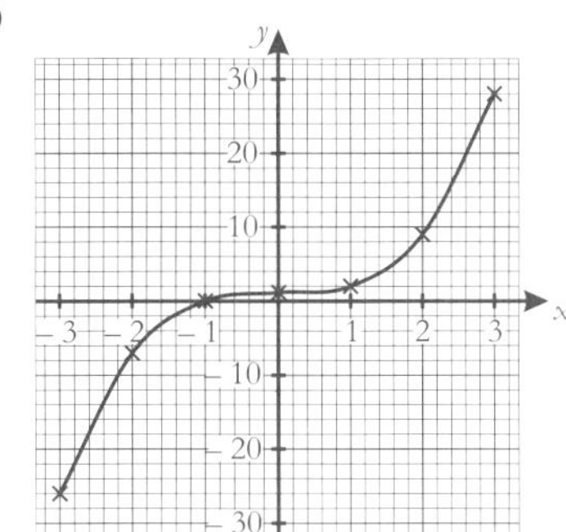

(b) $x = 2.1$ **(c)** $x = -1$ **(d)** $x = 2.7$

A62 **(a)**

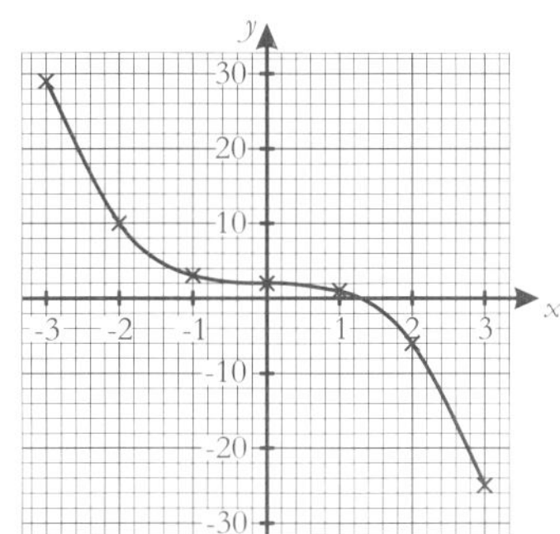

(b) $x = -2.6$ **(c)** $x = 1.3$ **(d)** $x = 2.3$

A63 8.2 m/s

A64 52 mph

A65 93 km

A66 1.536 km

A67 **(a)** Pippa

(b) 20 m (after 2 seconds)

(c) She stopped, perhaps after falling over.

(d) Pippa, she overtook Sarah.

A68 **(a)** 5 m/s

(b) 0.4 m/s^2 (gradient)

(c) 1200 m (area under the curve)

A69 **(a)** 16.25 m/s

(b) 0.03 m/s^2

(c) 1818.75 m

A70

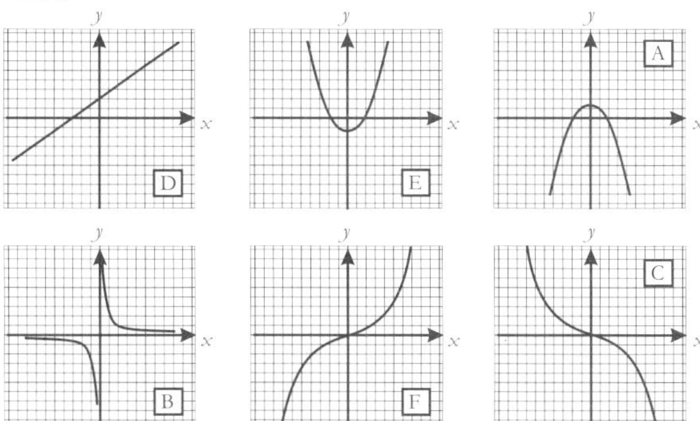

A71 Graph B cannot be $y = x^2 + 2$ because it cuts the y-axis at the origin, not at $y = 2$.

A72 A matches 4, B matches 3, C matches 2, D matches 1

A73 **(a)** Graph 1 **(b)** Graph 4

(c) Graph 2 **(d)** Graph 3

A74 **(a)**

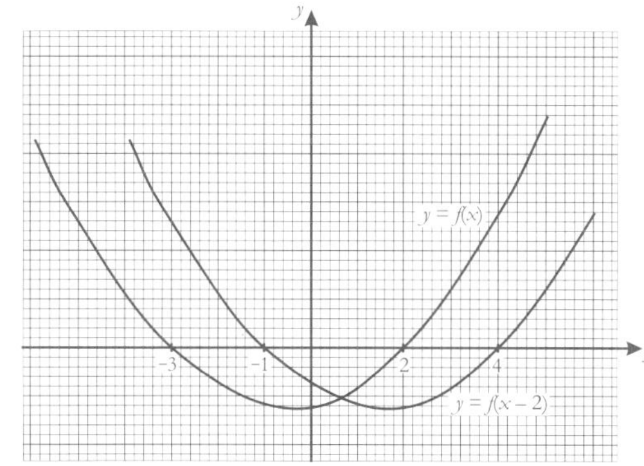

(b) (0, -18)

A75 **(a)**

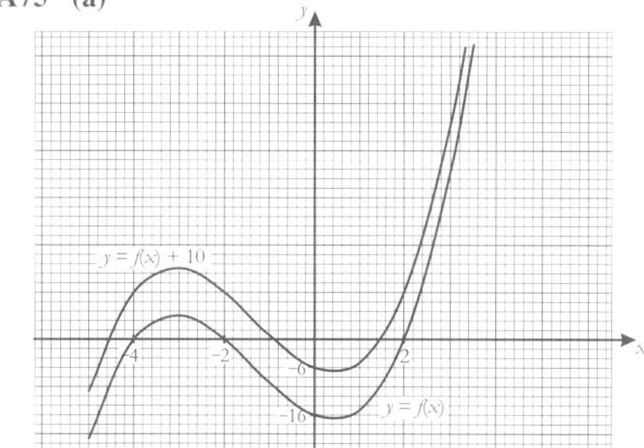

(b) $y = -x^3 + 4x^2 + 4x - 16$

A76 **(a)** $5 + (6 \times 7)$

(b) $n + (n + 1)(n + 2) = n^2 + 4n + 2$

A77 **(a)** $(7 \times 8)^2$

(b) $n^2(n + 1)^2 = n^4 + 2n^3 + n^2$

A78 **(a)** $n(n + 4)(n - 1)$

(b) $\dfrac{n(n + 4)(n - 1)}{2} + 2$

A79 **(a)** $\frac{1}{2}n^2(n - 3)^2$

(b) $n^2(n - 3)^2 - 4$

A80 **(a)** $5n - 3$

(b) $\frac{1}{2}n^2 - \frac{1}{2}n + 3$

A81 **(a)** $4n - 1$

(b) $n^2 - n + 5$

A82 **(a)** **(i)** $a = \frac{8}{6}b = 13\frac{1}{3}$ **(ii)** $b = \frac{6}{8}a = 49\frac{1}{2}$

(b)

x	50	8	$\frac{1}{2}$	2
y	2	5	20	10

A83 **(a)**

p	80	180	5	0
q	2	3	0.5	0

(b) **(i)** 40 minutes

(ii) 2 painters

Answers

Shape, Space & Measures

S1 32 cm²

S2 15 m²

S3 **(a)** 204.2 cm³ **(b)** 77.9 cm²

S4 26.9 cm

S5 6.0 cm

S6 2144.7 cm³

S7 15.5 cm

S8 A surface area is always length × length, whereas this formula is length × length × length, which is typical of a volume formula.

S9 **(a)** D: $V = 4rh^2 + r^3$

(b) D is the only formula where all the terms are length × length × length.

S10 **(a)** $x°$ and 60° are corresponding angles and so are equal.

(b) 60°

S11 **(a)** $a°$ and 50° are alternate angles and so are equal.

(b) 130°

S12 **(a)** $x°$ and 120° are supplementary angles and so add up to 180°.

(b) 120°

S13 **(a)** Angles at a point add up 360°, so $a° + 40° = 360°$.

(b) 140°

S14 A hexagon has 6 sides, so the sum of the interior angles is $(6 - 2) \times 180° = 720°$.
$x = (720° - 90° - 120° - 130° - 140°) \div 2 = 120°$

S15 $x = 110°$

S16 **(a)**

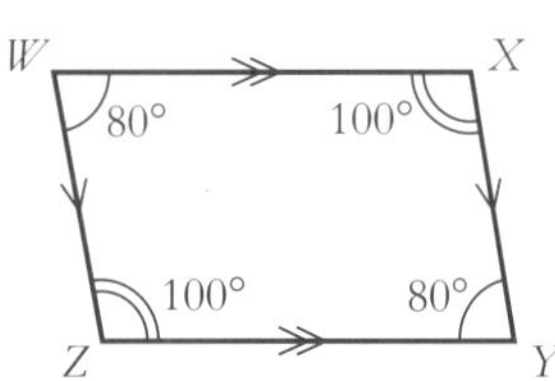

(b) 80°

S17 **(a)**

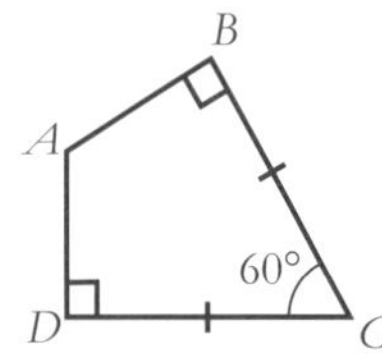

(b) 120°

S18 **(a)** 31.4 cm **(b)** 2.6 cm **(c)** 6.5 cm²

S19 **(a)** 9.5 cm **(b)** 60° **(c)** 168 cm²

S20 **(a)** 37.5° **(b)** 142.5°

S21 **(a)** 32° **(b)** 58°

S22 6.3 cm

S23 1204 m

S24 43°

S25 7.8 m

S26 **(a)**

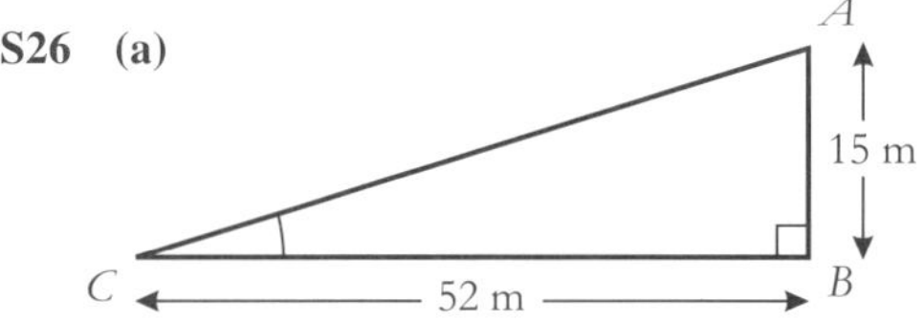

(b) 16.1°

S27 **(a)**

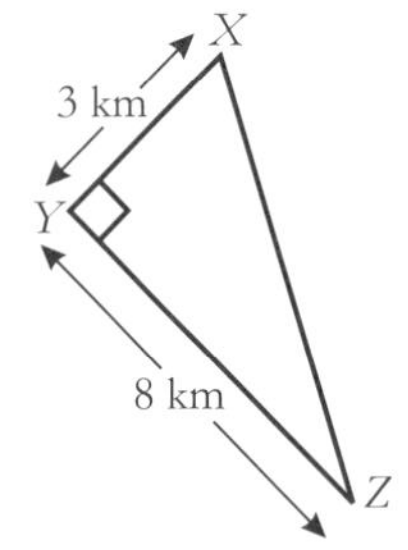

(b) 69.4° **(c)** 20.5° **(d)** 8.5 km

S28 34.6 cm

S29 **(a)** 28.4° **(b)** 72°

S30 **(a)** 14.1 cm **(b)** 69.3° **(c)** 37.4 cm

S31 **(a)** 70° **(b)** 5.5 cm **(c)** 11.6 cm

S32 **(a)**

(b) 210° and 330°

S33 78.46° and 281.54°

S34 **(a)**

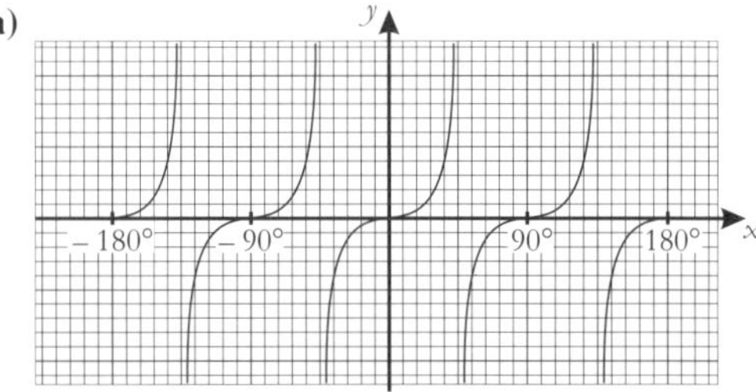

(b) -180°, -90°, 0°, 90°, 180°

S35 4.8 cm

S36 **(a)** 4.3 cm **(b)** 150°

S37 **(a)** $\begin{pmatrix} 6 \\ 2 \end{pmatrix}$ **(b)** $\begin{pmatrix} 6 \\ 7 \end{pmatrix}$

S38 **(a)** $\begin{pmatrix} -5 \\ 3 \end{pmatrix}$ **(b)** $\begin{pmatrix} 12 \\ -5 \end{pmatrix}$

S39 **(a)** **(i)** $\mathbf{a} + \mathbf{c}$ **(ii)** $\mathbf{a} - \mathbf{b}$

(b) $\mathbf{a} = \frac{1}{3}(\mathbf{b} - \mathbf{c})$

S40 **(a)** **(i)** $\mathbf{a} + \mathbf{b}$ **(ii)** $\mathbf{c} - \mathbf{a} - \mathbf{b}$

(b) $2\mathbf{a} - \mathbf{c} + \mathbf{b}$

S41 **(a)** Reflection in the x-axis

(b) Translation $\begin{pmatrix} -5 \\ 0 \end{pmatrix}$

S42 **(a)** 180° rotation about (4, 0)

(b)

(c) For example, 180° rotation about (-2, 0) followed by a reflection in the line x = -3.5. Many other combinations are possible.

S43 **(a)** & **(b)**

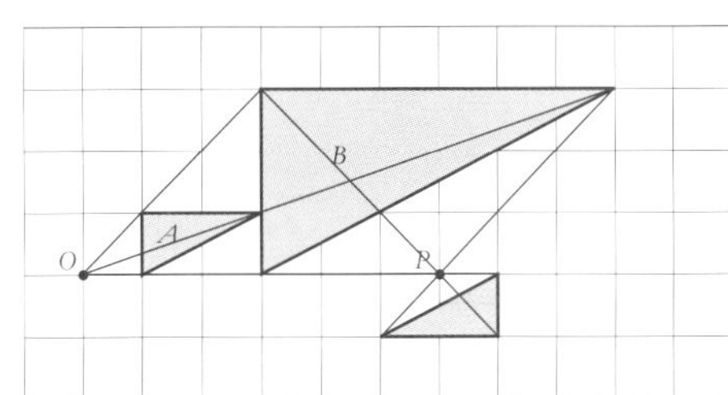

S44 **(a)** $\frac{1}{2}$

(b)

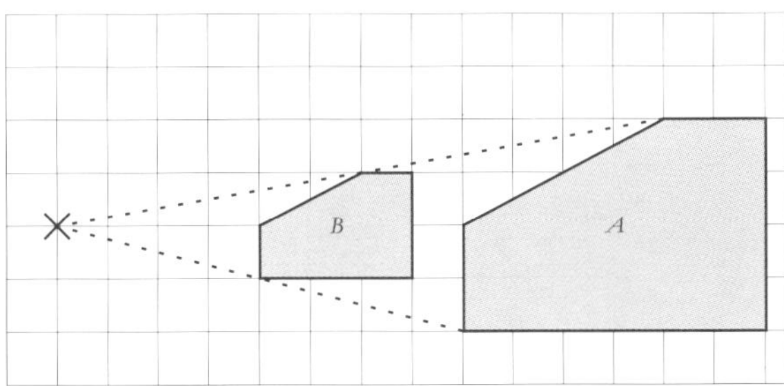

S45 **(a)** 2000 m

(b)

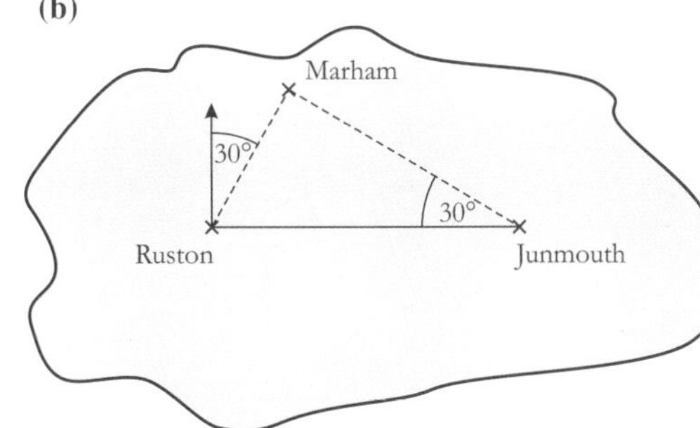

S46 **(a)** 600 m

(b)

S47 **(a)** 100°

(b)

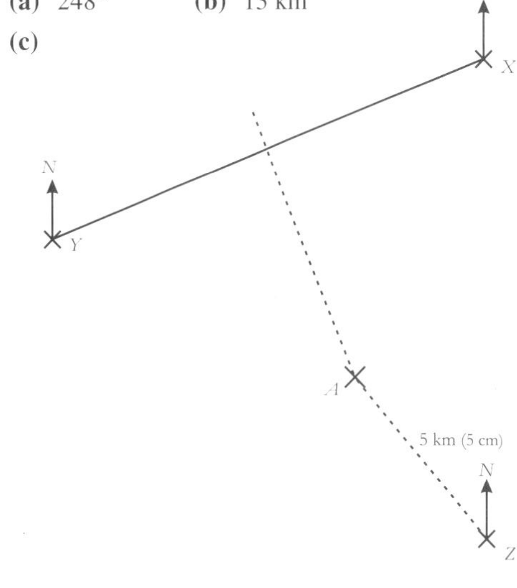

S48 **(a)** 248° **(b)** 13 km

(c)

S49

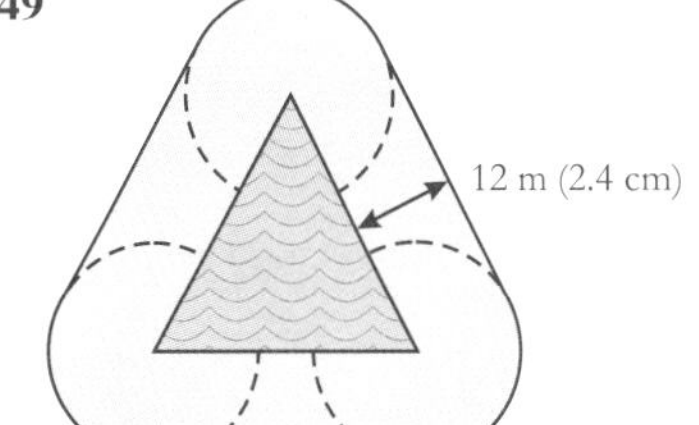

Answers

Shape, Space & Measures

S50

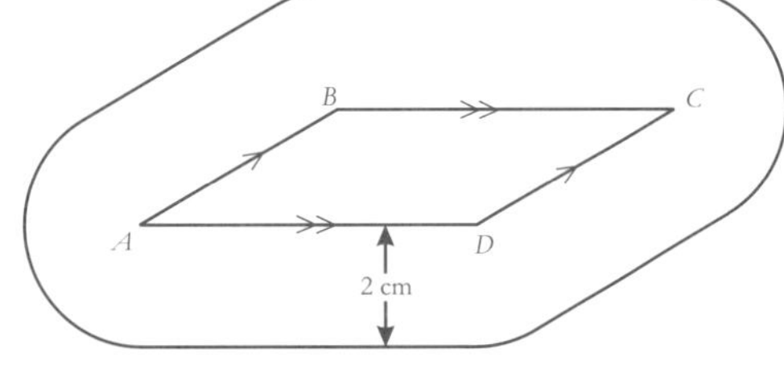

S51 **(a)** 32.495 kg **(b)** 32.485 kg

S52 **(a)** 52.45 m **(b)** 52.35 m

S53 Upper bound = $7.25 \times 4.55 = 32.9875$ cm^2
Lower bound = $7.15 \times 4.45 = 31.8175$ cm^2

S54 **(a)** $\frac{4.655}{2.45\pi} = \frac{1.9}{\pi}$ cm

(b) $\frac{1}{3}\pi \times 9.575^2 \times 2.425 = 74.1\pi$ cm^3

Handling Data

H1 **(a)** **(i)** 14 mm **(ii)** 87 mm

(b) The beef tomatoes are generally larger in diameter than the plum tomatoes, and are a more consistent size.

H2 **(a)** **(i)** 10 g **(ii)** 60 g

(b) Although the means are the same, the weights of the South African Green apples vary more.

H3 **(a)** 78 kg **(b)** 74 kg

(c) The mode, it's the lowest weight.

H4 **(a)** £546.63 **(b)** £56

(c) The mean does not give a good indication, it is distorted by an extreme value (£4002).

H5 **(a)**

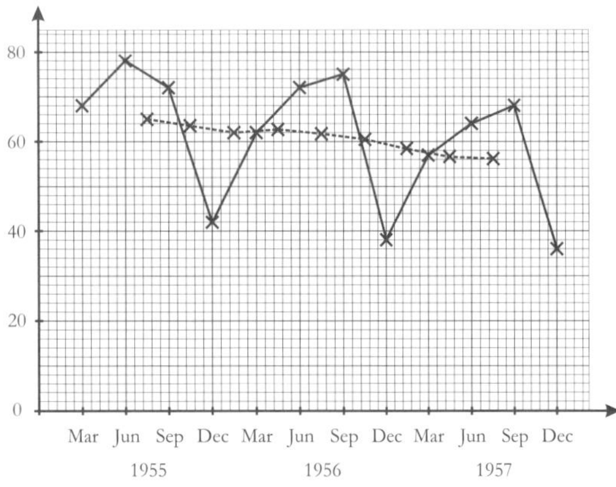

(b) The four-point moving averages are: 65, 63.5, 62, 62.75, 61.75, 60.5, 58.5, 56.75, 56.25

(c) The trend is slightly downwards, this could be due to falling sales or perhaps an increase in automation.

H6 **(a)** Mean = $54 \div 40 = 1.35$ goals

(b) Mode = 1 goal

H7 **(a)** 1.72 eggs **(b)** 1 egg **(c)** 1.5 eggs

H8 **(a)**

Height (h cm)	Tally	Frequency
$40 \leqslant h < 44$	||	2
$44 \leqslant h < 48$	~~||||~~	5
$48 \leqslant h < 52$	~~||||~~ ||	7
$52 \leqslant h < 56$	~~||||~~ ||	7
$56 \leqslant h < 60$	|||	3

(b)

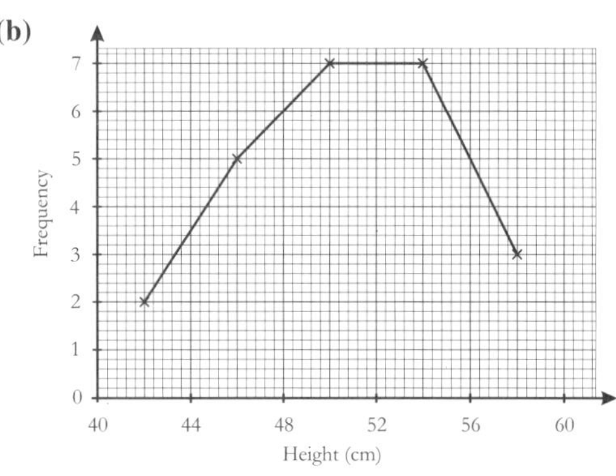

H9 **(a)**

Time (T mins)	Tally	Frequency
$30 \leqslant T < 36$	|||	3
$36 \leqslant T < 42$	~~||||~~	5
$42 \leqslant T < 48$	~~||||~~ ~~||||~~ |	11
$48 \leqslant T < 54$	~~||||~~ |||	8
$54 \leqslant T < 60$	|||	3

(b)

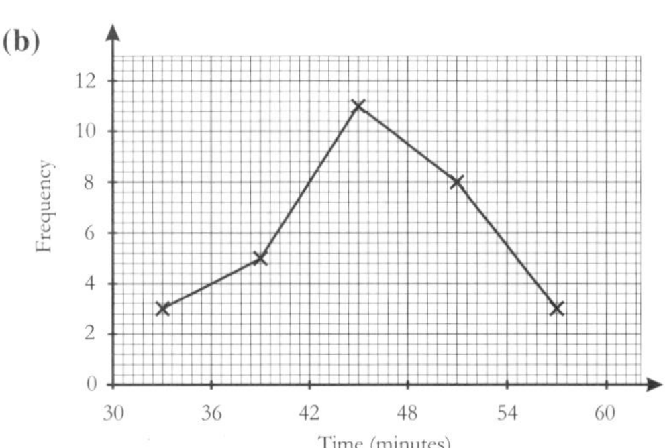

H10 **(a)** 40 people **(b)** 27 mins

(c) 30 people **(d)** 14 mins

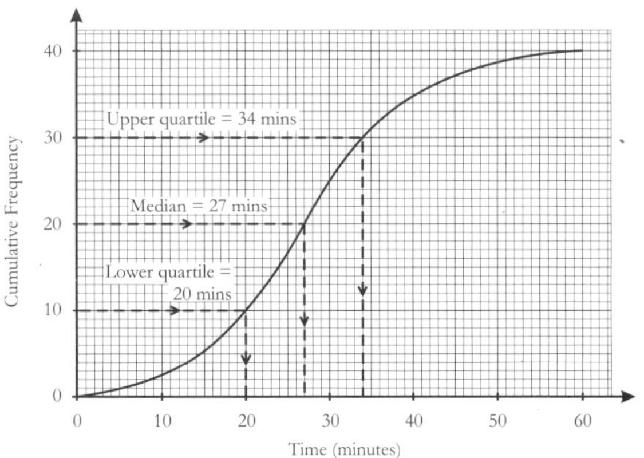

H11 **(a)** 60 families **(b)** £35

(c) 66.7% **(d)** £20

H12 (a)

£P less than	Number
500	0
550	4
600	34
650	84
700	180
750	230
800	240

(b)

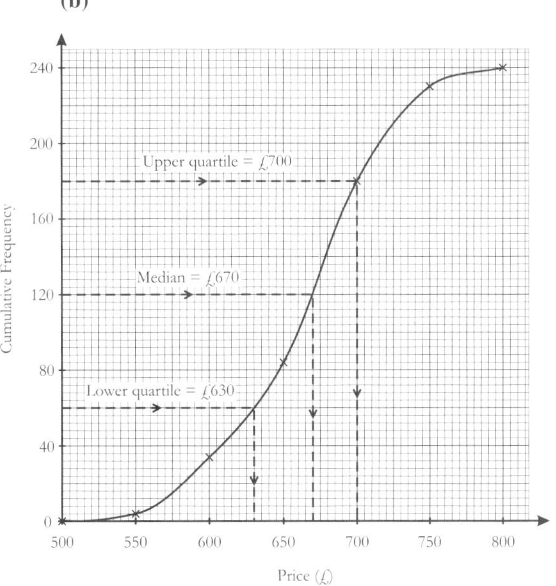

(c) **(i)** £670 **(ii)** £70

H13 (a)

Time (t mins)	Cumulative Frequency
t < 40	0
t < 50	8
t < 60	36
t < 70	100
t < 80	140
t < 90	155
t < 100	160

(b)

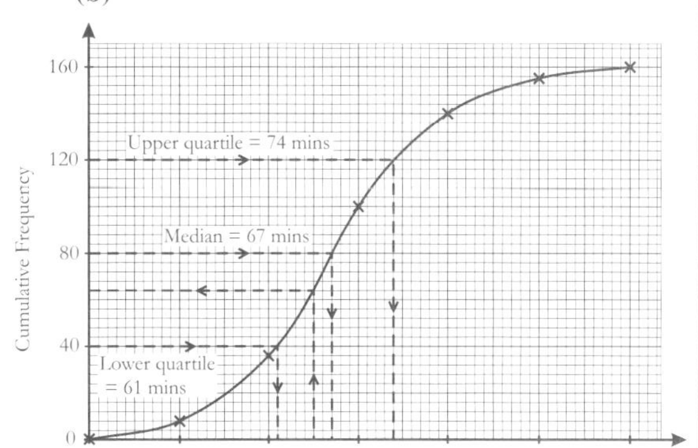

(c) 67 minutes

(d) 96 people

(e) 13 minutes

H14

	Time in seconds
Minimum	8
Maximum	53
Median	31
Lower quartile	26
Upper quartile	34

H15 **(a)**

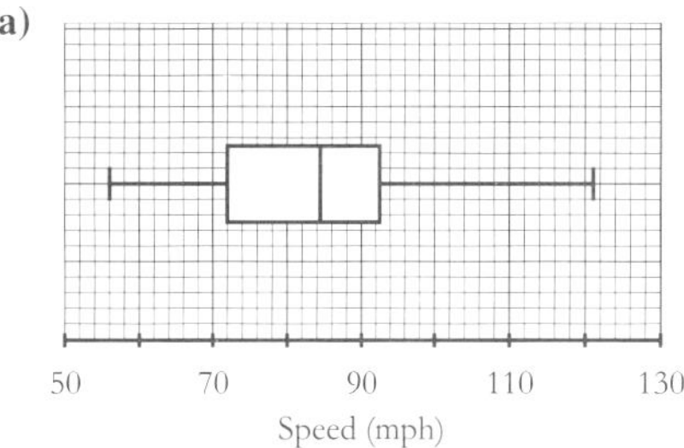

(b) The distribution is negatively skewed.

H16 **(a) & (c)**

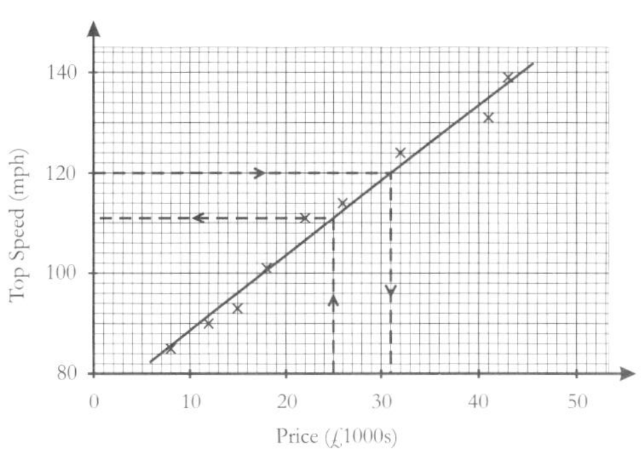

(b) Strong positive correlation

(d) **(i)** £31 000

(ii) 111 mph

H17 **(a)** & **(b)**

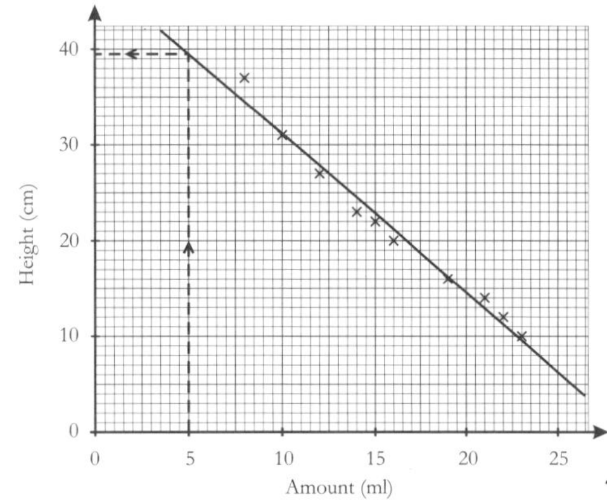

(c) 39.5 cm

(d) Strong negative correlation

H18 **(a)**

Time (t mins)	Frequency
$0 \leqslant t < 15$	10
$15 \leqslant t < 30$	20
$30 \leqslant t < 60$	40
$60 \leqslant t < 120$	20
$120 \leqslant t < 180$	10
$t > 180$	0

(b)

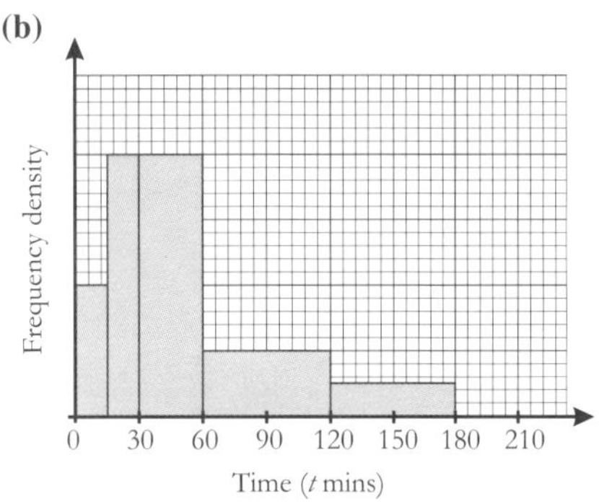

H19 **(a)**

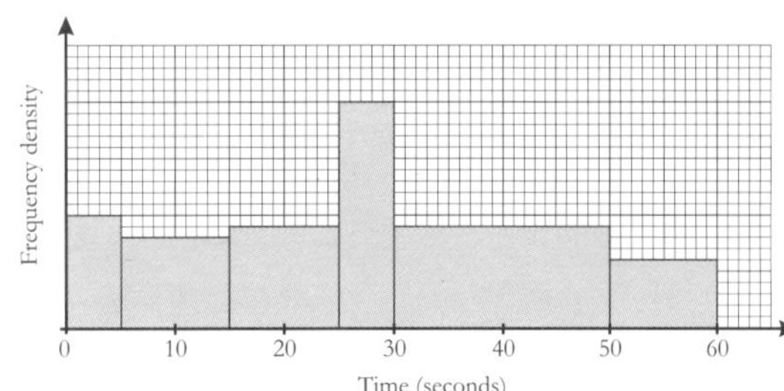

(b) 28.5 seconds

H20 **(a)** $\frac{19}{50}$ or 0.38 **(b)** $\frac{201}{500}$ or 0.402

(c) Use answer to **(b)**, as it is a better estimate than **(a)**. Spinner will land on A $0.402 \times 5000 = 2010$ times.

H21 **(a)** $\frac{62}{125}$ or 0.496 **(b)** $\frac{141}{500}$ or 0.282

(c) $\frac{3}{10}$ or 0.3

H22 **(a)** 0.7 **(b)** 0.5

H23 **(a)** 0.8 **(b)** 0.21 **(c)** 0.15

H24 **(a)** 0.0672 **(b)** 0.4872 **(c)** 0.5128

H25 **(a)** 0.03 **(b)** 0.97

H26 **(a)** $\frac{1}{66}$ **(b)** $\frac{1}{22}$ **(c)** $\frac{1}{99}$

H27 **(a)** $\frac{1}{6}$ **(b)** $\frac{1}{5}$ **(c)** $\frac{1}{20}$

H28 **(a)**

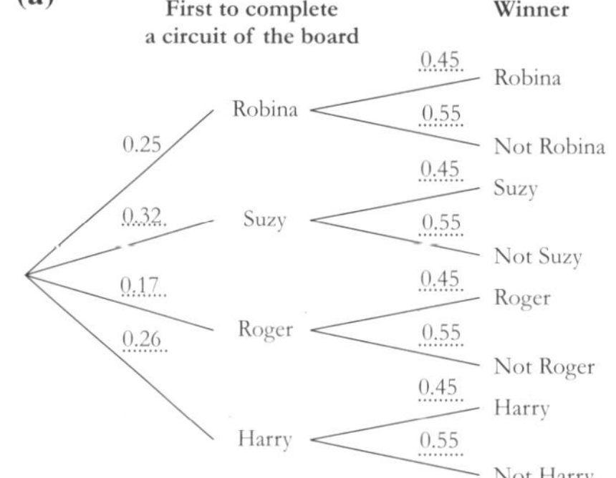

(b) $0.32 \times 0.55 = 0.176$

H29 **(a)**

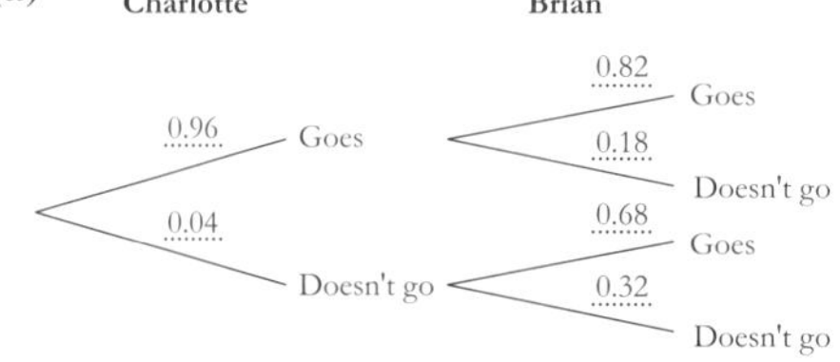

(b) 0.0272 **(c)** 0.9872

H30 **(a)** Cheaper/quicker than asking the whole population.

(b) It may not give a true reflection of the population.

(c) Stratified sampling is most suitable.

(d) The sample will give a good reflection of the area's views if households in every street are selected.

H31 **(a)** Any method where each member of the population is equally likely to be selected.

(b) Stratified sampling is most suitable.

(c) Divide the population into, for example, different age groups. Randomly select people from each age group (strata).